Air Force Physician and Dentist Multiyear Special Pay

Current Status and Potential Reforms

Edward G. Keating, Marygail K. Brauner, Lionel A. Galway,
Judith D. Mele, James J. Burks, Brendan Saloner

Prepared for the United States Air Force

Approved for public release; distribution unlimited

RAND PROJECT AIR FORCE

The research described in this report was sponsored by the United States Air Force under Contract FA7014-06-C-0001. Further information may be obtained from the Strategic Planning Division, Directorate of Plans, Hq USAF.

Library of Congress Cataloging-in-Publication Data is available for this publication.

ISBN 978-0-8330-4697-0

Published 2009 by the RAND Corporation
1776 Main Street, P.O. Box 2138, Santa Monica, CA 90407-2138
1200 South Hayes Street, Arlington, VA 22202-5050
4570 Fifth Avenue, Suite 600, Pittsburgh, PA 15213-2665
RAND URL: http://www.rand.org/
To order RAND documents or to obtain additional information, contact
Distribution Services: Telephone: (310) 451-7002;
Fax: (310) 451-6915; Email: order@rand.org

Preface

This monograph emanates from a RAND Project AIR FORCE study entitled "Optimizing Medical and Dental Officer Accession and Retention Incentives." This fiscal year (FY) 2008 study was jointly sponsored by the Director of Force Management Policy, Deputy Chief of Staff, Manpower and Personnel (AF/A1P), and the Assistant Surgeon General for Medical Force Development, Office of the Air Force Surgeon General (AF/SG1). The study's objective was to examine options for Air Force medical and dental officer incentive bonuses.

In the monograph, we present trends in accession, retention, and promotion in the Medical and Dental Corps and discuss Multiyear Special Pay (MSP) and observed tendencies of physicians and dentists to accept MSP. A series of estimations that we undertook to calibrate how physicians respond to higher MSP levels has been put into an appendix in the interest of streamlining the narrative flow of the body of the monograph.

Related RAND Corporation documents include the following:

- *Retention of Volunteer Physicians in the U.S. Air Force,* by Victoria L. Daubert (R-3185-AF), 1985.
- *I Want You! The Evolution of the All-Volunteer Force,* by Bernard Rostker (MG-265-RC), 2006.
- *The Dynamic Retention Model for Air Force Officers: New Estimates and Policy Simulations of the Aviator Continuation Pay Program,* by Michael Mattock and Jeremy Arkes (TR-470-AF), 2007.

This research is intended to be of interest to Air Force and other Department of Defense personnel involved with military personnel compensation policy and health affairs issues.

RAND Project AIR FORCE

RAND Project AIR FORCE (PAF), a division of the RAND Corporation, is the U.S. Air Force's federally funded research and development center for studies and analyses. PAF provides the Air Force with independent analyses of policy alternatives affecting the development, employment, combat readiness, and support of current and future aerospace forces. Research is conducted in four programs: Force Modernization and Employment; Manpower, Personnel, and Training; Resource Management; and Strategy and Doctrine. The research reported here was performed within the Manpower, Personnel, and Training Program.

Additional information about PAF is available on our Web site: http://www.rand.org/paf

Contents

Figures

Tables

Summary

Since the advent of the all-volunteer force, the U.S. military has struggled with how best to attract and retain physicians and dentists. As of September 30, 2007, there were approximately 3,400 physicians in the Air Force's Medical Corps and 900 dentists in its Dental Corps. Both populations have declined in recent years. The Air Force Medical Corps has had a pattern of decreasing annual accessions that dates back to 1990. Dental Corps accessions, however, have been variable from year to year.

The Air Force's three largest Medical and Dental Corps accession paths all involve sizable lags between an individual's commitment to serve in the Air Force and actual provision of trained medical or dental services. The foremost accession tool is the Health Professions Scholarship Program (HPSP), in which the military pays for medical or dental school tuition, books, and fees and provides a monthly stipend to the student in exchange for a one-for-one service commitment. A related accession program is the Financial Assistance Program (FAP), in which the military provides a stipend to a non-HPSP physician in a civilian residency program in exchange for postresidency military service by that physician. The Department of Defense also operates the Uniformed Services University of Health Sciences (USUHS) medical school. USUHS students do not pay tuition and receive a stipend while at USUHS but then owe a post-USUHS seven-year service commitment (not counting time spent in residency training).

Since 1975, Air Force Medical Corps annual attrition has generally been greater than Dental Corps attrition, but the opposite has been true in recent years. Medical Corps attrition has trended downward in recent years, while Dental Corps attrition (though highly variable from year to year) has trended upward. Our analysis suggests that the Medical Corps' downward population trend has largely been caused by accession reductions, while the Dental Corps' foremost recent challenge has been retention. (See pp. 7–8.)

Physicians and dentists in the military are officers. Along with the compensation that an officer of a given rank receives, Air Force physicians and dentists are eligible for a variety of special pays. These special pays include Additional Special Pay, Variable Special Pay, Board-Certified Pay, Incentive Special Pay, and MSP. MSP is the focus of this monograph. Under this program, qualifying physicians and dentists who make two-, three-, or four-year commitments to additional service receive additional annual payments. The Air Force asked RAND to describe the tendencies of physicians and dentists to accept MSP.

Trends in Accession, Retention, and Promotion in the Air Force Medical Corps (1976–2007)

We examined the service records of physicians in the Air Force Medical Corps from 1976 to 2007. Three major trends in Medical Corps accession sources are noteworthy. First, beginning in the early 1980s, HPSP produced the vast majority of physicians, 60–80 percent of all entrants. Second, direct accessions, who made up more than one quarter of all entrants in the first few years of the all-volunteer force, had virtually disappeared by the end of the study period. Third, USUHS emerged as a stable accession source, contributing just over 8 percent of all entrants in most years. (See pp. 16–17.)

The racial and gender composition of Air Force physicians has changed considerably over time, corresponding to the increased entry of females and minorities into both the civilian physician labor market and into the Air Force Officer Corps more broadly. (See pp. 18–21.)

The data suggest that many physicians retrained and upgraded their skills while in the Medical Corps. (See pp. 22–25.)

We also found that, in virtually every accession category, the majority of entering physicians did not stay beyond their minimum service obligations. The exception was USUHS graduates, who were just as likely to stay for more than 20 years as to leave after the end of their estimated minimum service obligations. For HPSP, the largest accession group, completing a military residency was associated with a roughly three times greater probability of staying for more than 20 years relative to those who had completed a civilian residency. (See pp. 23, 26.)

Beyond accession source, race and specialty were also correlated with retention. In particular, African Americans, Hispanics, and Native Americans stayed, on average, more than three years longer than did white non-Hispanic physicians (after controlling for accession source). More highly compensated specialties, such as surgery, obstetrics, and orthopedics, also tended to have shorter retentions than did general and internal medicine specialties. After controlling for residency length, the group with the longest retention was aerospace medicine physicians. This population was probably attracted to military service in the first place and sought a residency in a field that would allow for this kind of a career. The entering specialty with the highest 20-year retention rate was pediatricians. (See pp. 26–30.)

In general, physicians who pursued residencies in the military had much higher retention and also faster promotions. Graduates of the HPSP program who completed military residencies were promoted from both major to lieutenant colonel and from lieutenant colonel to colonel more quickly than their HPSP civilian residency counterparts. The underlying cause of this difference is not clear. (See pp. 31–35.)

To the extent that promotion speed differences might be attributable to behavioral differences in these populations, it could be a reflection of differences in commitment to military service of the two groups. The HPSP graduates who were more interested in civilian careers may have self-selected themselves into civilian residencies. An alternative, although not mutually exclusive, explanation is that military residencies helped transition physicians into the military's culture. Regardless of a physician's taste for military service when he or she was selecting a residency, those who entered military residencies had a greater opportunity to become acculturated to the expectations and roles of a physician in the Air Force Medical Corps.

Physician Cohort Analysis

To study physician predilection to accept MSP, we focused on entering cohorts of physicians. For instance, a physician would be in the 1989 entering cohort if his or her first Air Force service as a physician occurred during FY89.

While members of an entering cohort share their first year of service as Air Force physicians, intracohort heterogeneity remains considerable. Along with having different medical specialties, some members of an entering cohort have already completed civilian residency programs, while others are just starting military residency programs.

Physicians who enter Air Force service having already completed a civilian residency are typically just three or four years away from being eligible to leave the Air Force. By contrast, a physician whose first service is as a military resident is many more years away from fulfilling his or her service obligation, since years in a military residency do not count toward educational obligation fulfillment. Indeed, data confirm that physicians who enter the Air Force with completed residencies depart Air Force service at a much faster rate. (See pp. 39–40.)

To qualify for MSP, a physician must have

- completed appropriate residency training (civilian or military)
- at least eight years of creditable service OR completed any active duty service obligation incurred for medical education and training.

We estimated when individuals became eligible for MSP on a physician-by-physician basis. A typical physician entering cohort has two peaks of MSP eligibility attainment. The first peak occurs after three to four years when civilian residency–completing physicians fulfill their initial obligation to the Air Force. We label this population "early eligibles." The second peak occurs seven to eight years after entrance when military residency–completing physicians either fulfill their initial obligation or complete eight years of service. We label this population "later eligibles." "Later eligible" physicians have accepted MSP at much greater rates than "early eligible" physicians. There has, however, been an upturn in recent cohorts' early eligible MSP acceptance rates. (See pp. 44–47.)

Trends in Accession, Retention, and Promotion in the Air Force Dental Corps (1976–2007)

Unlike physicians, who have many different accession sources and specialties, Air Force dentists are a more homogeneous group. Most dentists during the study period were direct accessions (particularly in the early years that were the subject of the retention and promotion analyses). This trend was reversed toward the end of the study period, in which HPSP graduates became the most common accession source. Dentists also had fewer specialties than physicians; for the most part, the Dental Corps was dominated by generalists. Although generalists did predominate, many of them continued their training while in the Dental Corps. One-third to one-half of dentists who entered in a non-residency field left with a residency completed. (See pp. 49–55.)

The retention of dentists was relatively high. A dentist entering the Dental Corps at the beginning of the study period had a greater than 60-percent chance of staying for longer than three years, greater than 40-percent chance of staying for longer than seven years, and greater than 20-percent chance of staying for longer than 19 years. Over time, however, retention at every experience level decreased. The cause of this decrease is not clear. It does correspond to the entry of HPSP graduates, but this association is not necessarily causal. Decreased retention has led to a shrinking of the Dental Corps. (See pp. 54, 56–58.)

The retention of underrepresented minorities was somewhat higher than that of white non-Hispanic dentists. Women had lower observed retention, especially at seven years of service. (See pp. 58–60.)

Promotion for dentists followed quite predictable promotion points. Promotion from captain to major, major to lieutenant colonel, and lieutenant colonel to colonel each most often happened at six-year intervals. Consistent with this pattern, more than half of all colonels were promoted in their 18th year. We found some evidence of differential promotion by gender and race in the earlier cohorts. However, these findings were based on small samples and are not adjusted for entry year, so it remains an open question whether this association would hold with more careful statistical controls. (See pp 60–63.)

Because many of the retention and promotion findings in our analysis were restricted to entry years from 1978 to 1988 (to avoid truncation and censoring problems), they may not generalize to later cohorts.

Dentist Cohort Analysis

Dentists' responses to MSP opportunities have been very different from those of physicians. Conditional on becoming eligible for MSP, dentists have accepted such pay (the Dental Officer Multiyear Retention Bonus [DOMRB]) at much greater rates than physicians have. (See p. 65.) However, most Air Force dentists have not completed residencies that would make them eligible for MSP/DOMRB. (See p. 67.) While the DOMRB has had no clear effect on dentist attrition (which has been trending up), it has sharply reduced the percentage of Air Force dentists who are within one year of the expiration of their service commitment. (See pp. 69–70.)

Conclusions

In the short run, the major accession flows into the Air Force Medical and Dental Corps (HPSP, USUHS, and FAP) are predetermined. Therefore, if the Air Force wants to increase the Medical or Dental Corps populations, the only clear-cut short-run tactic would be to reduce the attrition rate of physicians and dentists whose service commitments are about to expire. (See p. 71.)

MSP is intended to keep physicians and dentists in the Air Force after their initial service obligations have expired. MSP has been successful in that eligible dentists, in particular, have often accepted it. Most eligible physicians have heretofore refused MSP, but physicians in some subpopulations, e.g., those who received residency training at military medical centers, have shown growing inclination to accept MSP. Increasing MSP levels appears to increase the percentage of physicians who choose to accept MSP rather than leaving Air Force service. (See p. 72.)

Both the Medical Corps and Dental Corps have had accession totals and attrition rates in recent years that will not sustain the corps' current sizes. Unless the Air Force wants these corps to continue to shrink, steps must be taken to either increase accessions or reduce attrition. (See pp. 72–74.)

We recommend the Air Force focus on increasing Medical Corps accessions. Still further increases in MSP could further reduce Medical Corps attrition, but the result would be an increasingly senior Medical Corps over time. If the Air Force wishes to maintain its current Medical Corps seniority structure, accessions must be increased or at least stabilized. (See pp. 73–74.)

We urge the Air Force to consider retention bonuses for dentists who have not yet completed residencies that make them eligible for DOMRB. Dental Corps accessions have been variable from year to year but have not shown the consistent diminution seen in the Medical Corps. DOMRB-eligible dentists are being retained at a high rate. The hole in the Dental Corps' portfolio lies in retaining dentists who have not completed DOMRB-qualifying residencies. (See p. 74.)

Table S.1 summarizes our findings and recommendations.

Table S.1
Summary of Findings and Recommendations

Category	Physicians	Dentists
Accessions	Trending downward	Static
Attrition	Near historic lows	Variable but trending up
Acceptance of MSP/DOMRB	Increased in recent years	About 50%, conditional on eligibility
Recommendation	Focus on increasing accessions	Increase retention incentives for dentists not eligible for DOMRB

Acknowledgments

The authors appreciate the assistance of personnel in our sponsors' offices: John Park, Lt Col Eric Johnson, Lt Col Helen Meisenhelder, Maj James Cordeiro, and Maj Todd Sriver of AF/A1 and Col Grant Hartup, Col Arynce Pock, Lt Col Thomas Cheatham, Maj Erica Auerbach, and Maj Kate Morganti of AF/SG1.

We benefited from an April 24, 2008, visit to the Air Force Personnel Center and the Air Force Recruiting Service at Randolph Air Force Base. There, we met with experts including Col Phillip Sandefur, Lt Col Stephen Greentree, Maj Risa Riepma, Capt (now Maj) Robert Corby, Gerald Ball, and Dayan Geiger.

Darlena Ridler and Matthew Torres of the Defense Manpower Data Center provided assistance with pay file data. Collins Mikesell of the American Association of Medical Colleges provided a valuable data extract to the authors. Denise Anderson of USUHS provided information on their students' backgrounds.

We received constructive reviews of an earlier draft of this document from Daniel Cohen of USUHS and our RAND colleague James Hosek. Cynthia Cook and Margaret Lada orchestrated the Project AIR FORCE document review process.

We appreciate the assistance of our RAND colleagues, including program director Al Robbert, deputy program director Bart Bennett, and former deputy program director Larry Hanser. Edward Chan and Christine Eibner noted relevant literature. Jack Graser provided a number of constructive suggestions that improved the document. Susan Hosek gave us a number of valuable insights about the military medical system. Craig Martin provided programming assistance and

Gary Massey provided insights on the data. Michael Mattock assisted in the estimations described in Appendix D. Laura Miller provided insight on female participation in the Air Force Officer Corps, and Ben Mundell gave us insights on Air Force career paths. Lt Col Hans Ritschard provided background on policies and career paths within the Medical Corps. Roberta Shanman, Tomiko Envela, and Brooke Hyatt provided literature search assistance. Jane Siegel helped prepare this document. Miriam Polon edited this document.

While this paper was being finalized, Al Robbert's administrative assistant, Susan Bowen, passed away. We miss her greatly.

Of course, any remaining errors are solely the authors' responsibility.

Abbreviations

ACOL	Annualized Cost of Leaving
ADSCD	Active Duty Service Commitment Date
AF	Air Force
AF/A1P	U.S. Air Force Deputy Chief of Staff, Manpower and Personnel, Director of Force Management Policy
AFPC	Air Force Personnel Center
AFSC	Air Force Specialty Code
AF/SG1	U.S. Air Force Surgeon General, Assistant Surgeon General for Medical Force Development
BFGS	Broyden-Fletcher-Goldfarb-Shanno
DAFSC	Duty Air Force Specialty Code
DMDC	Defense Manpower Data Center
DoD	U.S. Department of Defense
DOMRB	Dental Officer Multiyear Retention Bonus (the Dental Corps' version of MSP)
DOPMA	Defense Officer Personnel Management Act
DRM	Dynamic Retention Model
ENT	ear, nose, throat
FAP	Financial Assistance Program
FY	fiscal year

GPE	graduate professional education
HPSP	Health Professions Scholarship Program
MSP	Multiyear Special Pay
OB/Gyn	obstetrics and gynecology
PAF	Project AIR FORCE
PAFSC	Primary Air Force Specialty Code
USUHS	Uniformed Services University of Health Sciences

CHAPTER ONE

Introduction

Since the advent of the all-volunteer force, the U.S. military has struggled with how best to attract and retain physicians and dentists. Physicians and dentists are among our society's best-educated, highest-trained, and most highly compensated professionals, so attracting and retaining the desired number of physicians and dentists to military service is challenging.

Indeed, as noted by Bernard Rostker, concerns about physicians were one of the foremost arguments against the abolition of conscription.[1] In fact, the "last conscripts" in the U.S. military were some physicians with deferred service commitments that were eventually fulfilled in the late 1970s and early 1980s, long after 1973 (when conscription ended elsewhere in the military).

Air Force policymakers (and Department of Defense [DoD] policymakers, more generally) struggle with maintaining the Medical Corps (physicians) and Dental Corps (dentists). Each year, a number of physicians and dentists fulfill their obligation to serve in the Air Force. If Medical and Dental Corps' populations are to be maintained at desired end strength, skill mix, and experience levels, there must be enough accession of new physicians and dentists and/or retention of current physicians and dentists. Further complicating the challenge, complete reliance upon accessions is unlikely to be desirable because both the Medical and Dental Corps want a certain number of more

---

[1] Bernard Rostker, *I Want You! The Evolution of the All-Volunteer Force*, Santa Monica, Calif.: RAND Corporation, MG-265-RC, 2006.

senior, experienced officers to oversee and mentor officers new to Air Force service.

As of September 30, 2007, there were approximately 3,400 physicians in the Air Force's Medical Corps and 900 dentists in its Dental Corps. As shown in Figure 1.1, both populations have declined in recent years. The Medical Corps' post-1975 population peak was in 1992; it has fallen about 20 percent since then. The Dental Corps' post-1975 population peak was in 1983; it has fallen about 45 percent since then.

Figure 1.1 and many other results in this monograph come from annual (September) military personnel inventories supplied to RAND by the Air Force Personnel Center (AFPC). The most recent inventory used in this analysis was the September 30, 2007, inventory. These annual personnel inventories provide extensive information about the physicians and dentists in the Air Force, including the officer's rank, primary and duty Air Force specialty code (AFSC), active duty service commitment date (i.e., the date on which the officer's current service

Figure 1.1
Air Force Medical and Dental Corps Total Populations

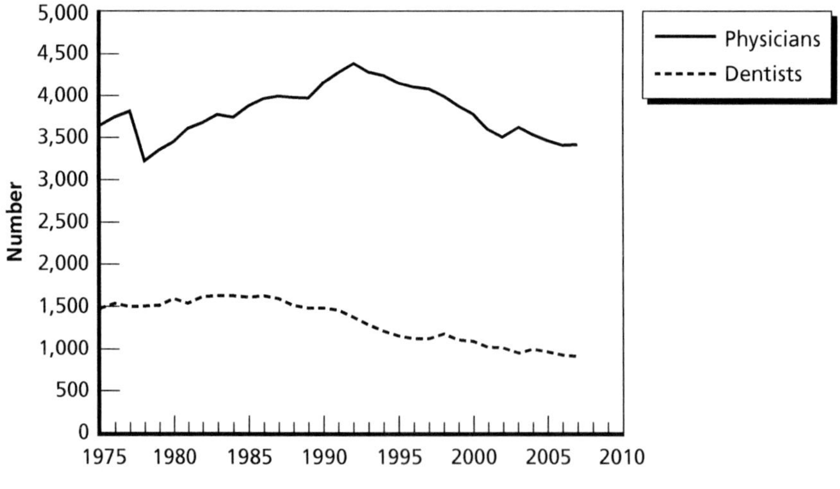

RAND *MG866-1.1*

obligation ends), accession source, and separation date (if the officer's Air Force service has ended).

Figure 1.2 shows the number of new accessions into the Air Force Medical and Dental Corps by fiscal year.[2]

Although 2006 and 2007 Medical Corps accessions were up slightly from 2005, the trend in Medical Corps accessions dating back to the early 1990s has been negative. Dental Corps accessions have

Figure 1.2
Air Force Medical and Dental Corps Annual Accessions

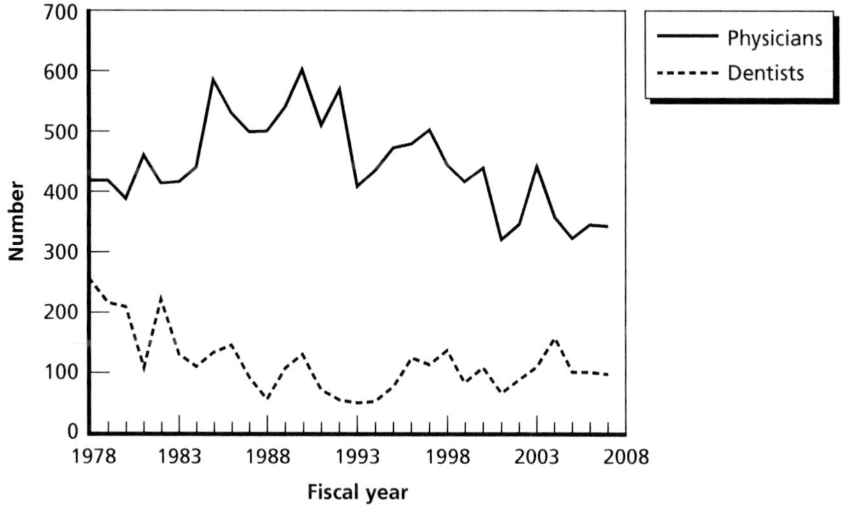

RAND *MG866-1.2*

---

2 Accessing into the Medical or Dental Corps is typically, but not always, the same as accessing into the Air Force. There are two common exceptions. First, Uniformed Services University of Health Sciences (USUHS) students appear in the personnel inventories as second lieutenants. We do not "count" them as being in the Medical Corps until they graduate from USUHS. Second, it is not unknown for an individual to have non–Medical Corps or Dental Corps Air Force service, e.g., as a pilot, leave the Air Force to attend a civilian medical or dental school, then return to the Air Force as a physician or a dentist. A third path is a combination of the first two, i.e., serving in the Air Force in a nonmedical capacity then attending USUHS. We only "count" such individuals when they begin Air Force service as a physician or dentist.

been variable from year to year, but they have not shown the post-1990 downward trend seen in Medical Corps accessions.

The Air Force's three largest Medical and Dental Corps accession paths all involve sizable lags between an individual's commitment to serve in the Air Force and actual provision of trained medical or dental services.

The foremost accession tool is the Health Professions Scholarship Program (HPSP), in which the military pays for medical or dental school tuition, books, and fees and provides a monthly stipend to the student, in exchange for a one-for-one service commitment (e.g., if the military paid for four years of medical school, the physician would owe four years of postresidency training service to the military).[3] According to AFPC data, Air Force HPSP physician accessions totaled 3,252 between 1991 and 2000. HPSP dental accessions totaled 296 between 1991 and 2000 but 566 between 2001 and 2007. A related accession program is the Financial Assistance Program (FAP), in which the military provides a stipend to a non-HPSP physician in a civilian residency program in exchange for postresidency military service by that physician.[4] Air Force FAP physician accessions totaled 506 between 1991

[3] The typical career path is for a new medical school graduate to receive further residency training for three to five years. That residency training can occur at a civilian medical center or as an officer at a military medical center. Upon completion of residency training, the physician must pass board certification examinations. If the physician served his or her residency at a civilian medical center, it is only upon completion of that residency that he or she would begin service as a military officer. Under either scenario, only years served postresidency count toward fulfillment of the HPSP obligation. Military residency years would, however, count toward military retirement eligibility if the physician served that long in the Air Force. Contrasting these two paths, HPSP physicians who receive residency training in civilian medical centers are referred to as "deferred" accessions, i.e., they enter military service later than their counterparts who receive residency training as an officer at a military medical center. HPSP dentists generally enter Air Force service upon dental school graduation and start fulfillment of their obligation either immediately or after a period of additional Air Force-provided training. See 10 U.S.C. 2123 and Tom Philpott, "Surgeon General: Looming Doctor Shortage," *Stars and Stripes*, July 13, 2006.

[4] A given individual cannot not be in both HPSP and FAP. If a physician had HPSP funding for medical school, he or she would either serve a residency at a military medical center (and typically receive the compensation associated with being an Air Force captain) or would serve a residency at a civilian medical center. Under the latter scenario, he or she would receive the (limited) compensation that the medical center pays all of its physicians in resi-

and 2000. FAP exists on only a limited scale for the Dental Corps; dentists generally enter military service without having yet commenced residency training. Levy, Christensen, and Asamoah explore enhancing FAP by giving larger payments to physicians in the program.[5]

The Department of Defense also operates the Uniformed Services University of Health Sciences (USUHS), a medical (but not dental) school located in Bethesda, Maryland. USUHS students do not pay tuition and receive a stipend while at USUHS but then owe a post-USUHS seven-year service commitment (not counting time spent in residency training).[6] The obligations of USUHS students are specified in 10 U.S.C. 2114. There has been controversy about the costs of operating USUHS; however, USUHS graduates make up a considerable share of the Air Force's more experienced physicians.[7] Both because of their longer initial service commitment and apparently greater inclination toward military service, USUHS-trained physicians have much longer military careers, on average, than is true of HPSP or FAP accessions. Cohen and colleagues discuss the careers of USUHS graduates.[8]

---

dency training, irrespective of whether the resident had an HPSP tie to the military. It is the limited compensation that civilian medical centers pay their residents that makes FAP's supplemental payments possibly alluring to a non-HPSP physician in residency training.

[5] Robert A. Levy, Eric W. Christensen, and Senanu Asamoah, *Raising the Bonus and the Prospects for DOD's Attracting Fully Trained Medical Personnel*, Alexandria, Va.: Center for Naval Analyses, CRM D0013237.A2/Final, February 2006.

[6] Rostker, 2006, discusses how the creation of USUHS was a political quid pro quo as part of the creation of the all-volunteer force.

[7] See, for instance, U.S. General Accounting Office, *Military Physicians: DOD's Medical School and Scholarship Program*, GAO/HEHS-95-244, September 1995, and Shayne Brannman, Eric W. Christensen, Ronald H. Nickel, Cori Rattelman, and Richard D. Miller, *Life-Cycle Costs of Selected Uniformed Health Professions (Phase II: The Impact of Constraints and Policies on the Optimal-Mix-of-Accession Model)*, Alexandria, Va.: Center for Naval Analyses, CRM D0007887.A2/Final, April 2003.

[8] Daniel L., Cohen, Steven J. Durning, David Cruess, and Richard MacDonald, "Longer-Term Career Outcomes of Uniformed Services University of the Health Sciences Medical School Graduates: Classes of 1980–1989," *Military Medicine*, Vol. 173, No. 5, 2008.

USUHS Air Force physician accessions totaled 454 between 1991 and 2000.[9]

USUHS accessions are more likely than other types of accessions to have prior Air Force active duty non–Medical Corps experience. Figure 1.3 shows the percentage of Medical Corps accessions who had prior active duty Air Force service before entering the Medical Corps (not counting time spent as a student at USUHS).[10]

Figure 1.3
Percentage of Accessions with Prior Active Duty Non–Medical Corps Air Force Experience

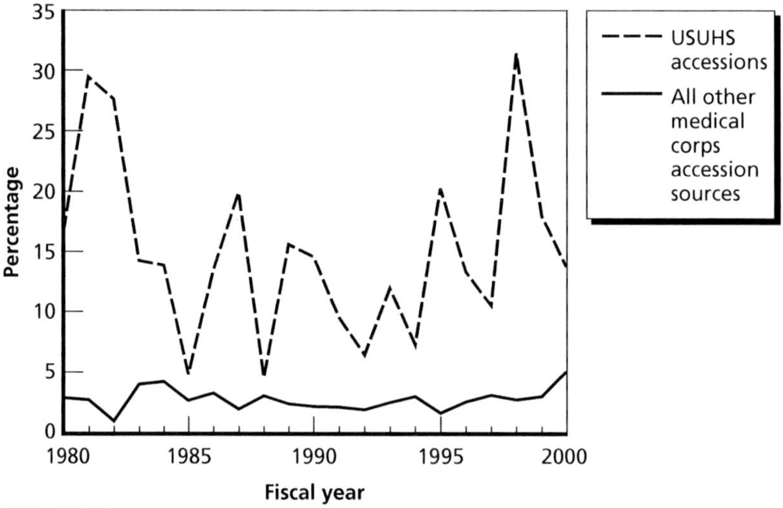

RAND *MG866-1.3*

---

[9] Unfortunately, we have found accession source codes to be unreliable since 2001, especially for FAP and USUHS. The Air Force transitioned to the MilPDS system in September 2001. Experts with whom we talked at the Air Force Personnel Center indicated they experienced "wholesale data failure" during that transition, though we do not know if the accession code problems we encountered were caused by that transition. Fortunately, our analysis largely focuses on physicians and dentists who entered Air Force service before 2001 so we believe their records to be more accurate.

[10] Figure 1.3 is not a complete tabulation of prior military service by Air Force Medical Corps accessions. It does not consider reserve service or service in branches of the military other than the Air Force. Also if, for instance, an individual went directly from the Air Force Academy to USUHS, without intervening active duty Air Force service, he or she would not be tallied as having had prior active duty Air Force service.

Looking across Medical Corps entering cohorts between 1980 and 2000, we see that about 14 percent of USUHS accessions had prior active duty Air Force non–Medical Corps service (before starting USUHS), whereas fewer than 3 percent of other types of accessions (e.g., HPSP, FAP) had prior active duty Air Force service, according to the AFPC personnel data. The percentage of USUHS accessions with prior active duty Air Force experience varied considerably from cohort to cohort, partly because the entering cohort sizes were fairly small. The number of USUHS accessions averaged about 45 per year between 1985 and 2000; the average number of accessions from all other sources averaged about 450 per year over the same period.

At any point in time, hundreds of future Air Force physicians and dentists are in the pipeline, working their way toward Air Force service. The flow of this pipeline into Air Force service within the next few years has already been determined. Improving HPSP benefits, for instance, might increase the number of new medical school students starting into the pipeline, but the impact of those individuals on the Air Force might be seven to eight years away. Since FAP participants are, by definition, closer to residency completion, their impact on the Air Force is closer at hand—perhaps three to four years distant.

Supplementing the three largest accession paths (HPSP, FAP, and USUHS) are a small number of fully trained and fully qualified physicians and dentists who join (or, in many cases, rejoin) the Air Force each year.[11]

At the other end of physicians' and dentists' Air Force careers, Figure 1.4 shows the Corps' annual attrition rates. These attrition rates are unfiltered, i.e., they are simply the percentage of physicians and dentists in the Air Force at the beginning of a fiscal year who depart by the next annual inventory. This tabulation does not consider the per-

---

[11] Since 1993, the number of physicians whose accession source code is "direct appointment through the recruiting service" has ranged from 0 (2003) to 26 (1996). Direct appointment physician accessions totaled 264 between 1991 and 2000. Numbers were greater in this accession code in the 1970s and 1980s with a peak of 143 "direct appointment" physicians in 1990. Dental Corps direct appointments totaled 527 between 1991 and 2000, but only 94 between 2001 and 2007.

Figure 1.4
Annual Attrition Rates, Medical and Dental Corps

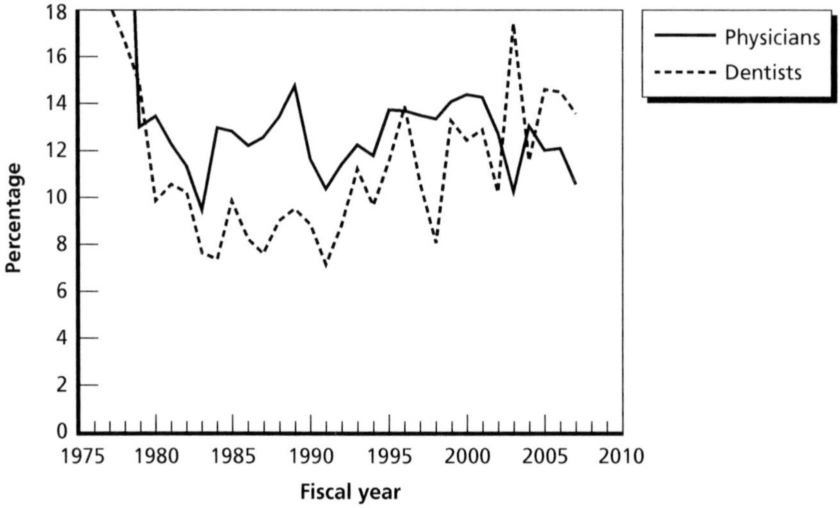

RAND *MG866-1.4*

centage who fulfilled their service commitment and hence were eligible to leave.

In most years, Medical Corps attrition was greater than Dental Corps attrition, but the opposite has been true in recent years: Medical Corps attrition has trended downward, whereas Dental Corps attrition (though highly variable from year to year) has trended upward. The 2007 Air Force Medical Corps attrition rate of 10.6 percent was lower than in any year of the all-volunteer force except 1983, 1991, and 2003.

Combined, Figures 1.1, 1.2, and 1.4 suggest that the Medical Corps' downward population trend has largely been caused by accession reductions, whereas the Dental Corps' foremost recent challenge has been retention.

We next discuss the financial compensation received by Air Force physicians and dentists. Although other factors also affect accession (e.g., recruiting resources, advertising) and retention (e.g., quality of life, danger, deployment policies), the financial compensation offered to physicians and dentists is clearly important. Financial compensation is also a readily altered policy lever compared with, say, whether and to what extent Air Force physicians and dentists are deployed to hostile settings. Not surprisingly, therefore, Air Force policymakers devote considerable attention to physician and dentist compensation policies.

Physician Compensation

Physicians in the military are officers. Along with the regular compensation (salary, allowances, benefits, eligibility for a military retirement after 20 years of service) that an officer of a given rank receives, Air Force physicians are eligible for a variety of special pays. In this section, we discuss the Fiscal Year (FY) 2009 (FY09) values of these special pays. These values are presented with more historical detail in Appendix B.

Any medical officer who is not undergoing initial residency training receives "Additional Special Pay" of $15,000 per year in FY09. The officer must sign a written agreement to remain on active duty for at least one year. (This Additional Special Pay has been fixed at $15,000 since 1990, so its inflation-adjusted value has declined considerably over time.)[12]

Physicians also receive "Variable Special Pay" of $1,200–$12,000 annually in FY09, with the level varying with the physician's years of creditable service to the DoD. Intriguingly, the Variable Special Pay apogee of $12,000 per year is attained for physicians with at least six, but less than eight, years of service. Variable Special Pay then declines with seniority down to $7,000 per annum for a physician with more than 22 years of creditable service.

Board-certified physicians receive additional "Board-Certified Pay" of $2,500–$6,000 in FY09. Board-Certified Pay, unlike Variable Special Pay, is greatest for those physicians with the most years of creditable service.

In FY09, physicians also receive "Incentive Special Pay" of $20,000–$36,000 annually, with the amount varying with a physi-

---

[12] See *Uniformed Services Almanac*, Falls Church, Va.: Uniformed Services Almanac, Inc., 1990, p. 21.

cian's specialty. While not as static over time as Additional Special Pay, Incentive Special Pay levels have been largely fixed in nominal terms in recent years. Some specialties (e.g., neurosurgeons, general surgeons, anesthesiologists, orthopedic surgeons) receive an augmentation to their Incentive Special Pay level when they sign a multiyear retention agreement.[13] These augmentations ranged from $0 (for a number of specialties, e.g., family practice, internal medicine, pediatricians) to $24,000 (neurosurgeons) in FY09.

Multiyear Special Pay (MSP) is the focus of this monograph. Under this program, qualifying physicians who make two-, three-, or four-year commitments to additional service receive annual payments that can reach $84,000 in FY09 (although the $38,000 MSP received by family practice physicians making four-year commitments in FY09 is more representative). MSP levels are lower for physicians who make two- or three-year additional service commitments. They also vary with a physician's specialty. The purpose of MSP is to retain personnel with desired medical skills and experience beyond their minimum service obligation.

As one might expect, specialists who might receive a greater civilian salary (e.g., neurosurgeons) tend to receive greater levels of MSP. Additionally, the Air Force can tailor the MSP program based on current and projected needs. For instance, no four-year commitment special pay was offered to Air Force pediatricians in FY08.[14]

The level of physician MSP has varied greatly over time. While Additional Special Pay, Variable Special Pay, and Board-Certified Pay levels have languished in nominal terms and degraded in inflation-

---

[13] In our estimation procedures, we tabulate such multiyear Incentive Special Pay augmentations as part of a physician's MSP. It is an increase in compensation received because the physician chose to sign a multiyear contract to continue his or her Air Force service. Hence, for our purposes, it "counts" as MSP, not Incentive Special Pay.

[14] The levels of MSP and other special pays are coordinated DoD-wide. An individual military service's only discretion is whether or not to offer the stipulated payment. The Air Force chose not to offer the DoD-prescribed $25,000 pediatrician four-year special pay level in FY08. The Air Force was not allowed to offer a pediatrician a four-year special pay of less than $25,000.

adjusted terms, MSP has been the bonus category the Air Force and the DoD have chosen to adjust considerably in recent years.

A physician can qualify for yet other types of additional compensation—for example, hostile fire and imminent danger pay if he or she was in a combat zone, flight pay for flight surgeons. The variety of bonuses a given physician can receive is daunting. Indeed, it is a noteworthy human resource management achievement to manage such a complicated compensation system.

Consider, for instance, a board-certified family practice physician (AFSC 44F3) with ten years of creditable service. Along with the standard compensation he or she would receive as a major or lieutenant colonel, the physician would also receive $15,000 in Additional Special Pay, $20,000 in Incentive Special Pay, $11,000 in Variable Special Pay, and $3,500 in Board-Certified Pay, summing to $49,500 in special pay in FY09. If the physician made a multiyear service commitment, he or she would also receive $17,000 (two-year commitment), $25,000 (three-year commitment), or $38,000 (four-year commitment) in annual MSP. There could be yet further additional compensation if the physician were deployed.

Dentist Compensation

Like physicians, dentists in the military are officers. Any dentist receives Additional Special Pay of $10,000–$15,000 in FY09, with the highest level for dentists with ten or more years of creditable service. Oral surgeons receive Incentive Special Pay of $30,000 per year in FY09, but no other type of dentist receives incentive special pay. Dentists receive Variable Special Pay of $3,000–$12,000, with the highest Variable Special Pay for dentists with eight to twelve years of creditable service. Board-certified dentists receive annual Board-Certified Pay of $2,500–$6,000.

Some dentists who stay in the Air Force pursue advanced residency training; some do not. A dentist's decision to pursue additional residency training is an important one from a compensation perspective because dentists who have not completed "qualifying residencies" are not eligible for Dental Officer Multiyear Retention Bonuses (DOMRBs), which are dentists' version of MSP.[15] Whereas the vast majority of physicians complete residencies that make them eligible for MSP, fewer than half of Air Force dentists ever complete such qualifying residencies. The level of DOMRB varies both with the dentist's specialty and the duration of service commitment (two, three, or four years) the dentist makes.

As an example of dental compensation, a board-certified comprehensive dentist (AFSC 47G3A) with ten years of creditable service would receive $15,000 in Additional Special Pay, $12,000 in Variable Special Pay, and $3,500 in Board-Certified Pay, summing to $30,500 in special pay in FY09. (A comprehensive dentist does not qualify for Incentive Special Pay.) If the dentist made a multiyear service commitment, he or she would be eligible for $25,000 (two-year commitment), $38,000 (three-year commitment), or $50,000 (four-year commitment) in DOMRB.

The remainder of this paper is structured as follows: Chapter Two provides an overview of accession, retention, and promotion patterns in the Air Force Medical Corps utilizing AFPC data from 1976 to 2007. Chapter Three focuses more directly on the issue of physician MSP. Different physician entering cohorts are defined and the predilection of those cohorts' physicians to accept MSP is described. Chapter Four is the dentists' version of Chapter Two, an overview of accession, retention, and promotion in the Air Force Dental Corps utilizing AFPC data from 1976 to 2007. Chapter Five provides a cohort analysis of dentists' predilection to accept MSP. Dentists accept MSP at much higher rates than physicians do, conditional on becoming eligible for it. But

[15] A *qualifying residency* is additional training a physician or dentist receives that allows him or her to specialize. A regular dental officer having just completed dental school could practice dentistry, but would have to turn some types of work (e.g., orthodontia, oral surgery, periodontics) over to a specialist. Dental careers are quite different from medical careers. Virtually all physicians complete residencies, typically immediately after completion of medical school. By contrast, many dentists, both within the military and in the civilian sector, never obtain further academic training after completion of dental school. Without the specialized training obtained in a "qualifying residency," a military dentist will not be eligible for DOMRB.

the majority of Air Force dentists never complete the residency training required for MSP eligibility. Chapter Six presents our conclusions.

The monograph additionally provides four appendixes. Appendix A discusses the procedure we used to estimate a physician's or dentist's eligibility for MSP. Appendix B provides a consolidated tabulation of Air Force medical and dental special pays between 1992 and 2009. Appendix C presents logistic regression analysis of physician MSP acceptance in which we estimate how the rate of MSP acceptance increases with the level of MSP. Finally, Appendix D discusses an attempt to use the Dynamic Retention Model to study physicians' decisions to accept or reject MSP.

CHAPTER TWO

Trends in Accession, Retention, and Promotion in the Air Force Medical Corps, 1976–2007

In this chapter, we examine some of the patterns in physician accession, retention, and promotion for entering cohorts from 1976 to 2007. The main data resource is AFPC's annual military personnel inventories, the latest of which was as of September 30, 2007. In total, the data file contains records for 15,012 physicians whom we observe entering the Air Force Medical Corps between October 1975 and September 2007.[1] For physicians in entering cohorts prior to the 1990s, the longer time series allows us to observe long-term outcomes, such as promotions later in the physician's career and retention after the physician became eligible for a military pension (after 20 years of service).[2] Utilizing this longer time series also allows us to examine variation within and across cohorts, providing a rich picture of changing service patterns over time.

---

[1] An additional 4,661 physicians who entered prior to October 1, 1975, were omitted from the analysis because an exact entry year could not be determined.

[2] Typically, an individual in our data would have to serve as a physician or dentist on active duty for 20 years to be eligible for a military retirement. The exceptions would be officers like those depicted in Figure 1.3 who had active duty military service prior to becoming physicians or dentists. Such individuals would therefore require fewer years of active duty service as physicians to retire. For expositional simplicity, we focus in this chapter (and in Chapter Four) on the fraction of officers who serve 20 years on active duty as Air Force physicians or dentists.

Patterns in Medical Corps Accessions

By following entering cohorts going back to FY 1976, we have the opportunity to examine some of the first cohorts of physicians who entered the Air Force after conscription ended in 1973. The cohorts of physicians in the beginning of the "all-volunteer" era differed from later cohorts in their modes of accession and background. As noted in Chapter One, procuring and retaining physicians was one of the major challenges the Air Force faced after the end of conscription. To obtain sufficient numbers of physicians, the Air Force relied heavily on direct accessions in the mid- and late-1970s, i.e., physicians who entered Air Force service fully qualified and trained without having received financial assistance from the Air Force prior to entrance. Graduates of the HPSP began to enter the Air Force in the mid-1970s, but HPSP accessions did not account for the majority of entrants until the 1980s. USUHS entrants first arrived in the early 1980s. Direct accessions were considered to be a less reliable accession source than HPSP and USUHS graduates, who carried longer service obligations upon entrance. Further, recruiting physicians with the adequate level of training and in the optimal mix of specialties was a major challenge. Direct-accession physicians were more likely to be graduates of foreign medical schools and less likely to be board-certified.[3]

Figure 2.1 shows the changing accession source composition of entering physician cohorts from 1978 to 2000.[4] In addition to HPSP and USUHS, we present trends for direct accessions and for FAP, a program that began in the late 1980s to provide stipend support during residency. Entrants with other modes of accession, including interservice transfers and those who had entered the Air Force through ROTC, are included in an "Other" category.

---

[3] Victoria L. Daubert, *Retention of Volunteer Physicians in the U.S. Air Force*, Santa Monica, Calif.: RAND Corporation, R-3185-AF, 1985.

[4] We omit cohorts from 2001 to 2007 due to problems we had with the accession source data field in Air Force personnel file. See Chapter One, footnote 9.

Figure 2.1
Changing Accession Sources of Medical Corps Entrants, 1978–2000

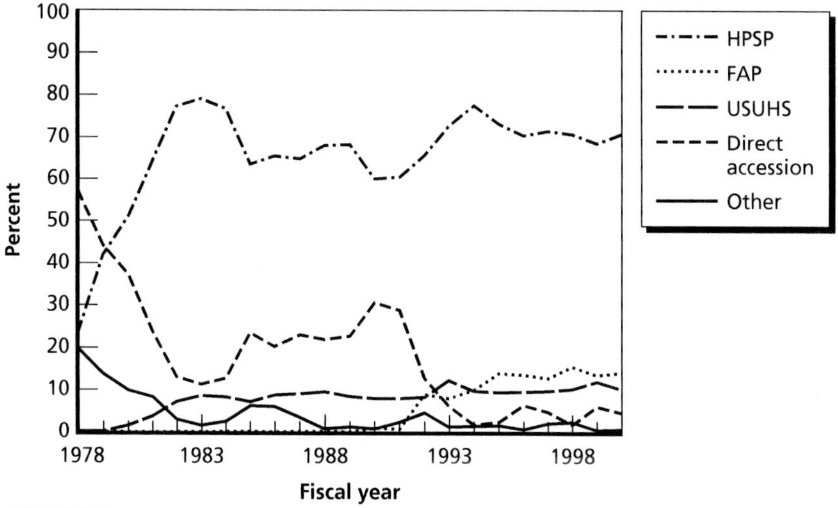

RAND *MG866-2.1*

Three major trends in Medical Corps accession sources are noteworthy. First, beginning in the early 1980s, HPSP produced the vast majority of physicians, between 60–80 percent of all entrants. Second, direct accessions, who made up more than one-quarter of all entrants in the first few years, had virtually disappeared by the end of the study period. Third, USUHS emerged as a stable accession source, contributing just over 8 percent of all entrants in most years.

In addition to changing accession sources, two other factors indirectly shaped the labor market for Air Force physicians during the study period. The first was changing conditions in the civilian labor market. The period from 1975 to 2007 was a time of tremendous increase in the supply of new physicians in this country. In 1970, there was one physician per 599 people in the United States. By 2000, the ratio had increased 44 percent to one physician per 384 people in the nation. Growth of the physician workforce was broadly spread across different specialty areas.[5] An increase in the supply of physicians did not

5 See U.S. Department of Health and Human Services (DHHS), Health Resources and Services Administration, National Center for Health Workforce Analysis, Web page, undated,

necessarily cause a decrease in their wages, but was likely mediated by changes in the organization and reimbursement of health care, including the rise of health maintenance organizations.[6] It is difficult to generalize about trends in physician wages because there was considerable variation in reimbursement and income across specialty areas and regions.

The second factor affecting the size of the Air Force physician population during the period was a reduction in the overall size of the Air Force's active duty population. After a slight buildup in force size during the early 1980s, the force was cut dramatically in the post–Cold War era beginning in the late 1980s and continuing into the 1990s. The active duty force size fell to about 350,000 in 2001, increased to about 370,000 in 2004, and fell to about 330,000 in 2007. Overall the force decreased by 61 percent from 1975 to 2007. By comparison, the size of the Air Force physician population experienced a net increase of six percent from 1978 to 2007. The physician-to-airmen ratio reached one physician for every 100 airmen in 1994 and remained near that level every year thereafter. This point is shown as the intersection of the two curves in Figure 2.2, which presents the annual counts of all Air Force active duty personnel as well as Air Force physicians (note that the two curves are scaled on different vertical axes that vary by a factor of one hundred). Figure 2.2 does not show the total beneficiary population—for example, it excludes dependents and retirees.

The racial and gender composition of Air Force physicians also changed considerably over time, corresponding to increased entry of

---

Table 202: Number of Active Physicians (MDs) and Physician-to-Population Ratios by Specialty, Selected Years 1970–2000.

[6] William B. Weeks and Amy E. Wallace, "Time and Money: A Retrospective Evaluation of the Inputs, Outputs, and Incomes of Physicians," *Archives of Internal Medicine*, Vol. 163, No. 8, 2003. The authors find that from 1987 to 1998 physician wages grew in inflation-adjusted terms for every specialty area but obstetrics. Using a financial returns methodology, the same authors find that the return on investment in graduate medical education was decreasing for specialties and increasing for primary care in the 1990s. See also William B. Weeks and Amy E. Wallace, "Long-Term Financial Implications of Specialty Training for Physicians," *American Journal of Medicine*, Vol. 113, No. 5, 2002.

Figure 2.2
Annual Medical Corps and Air Force Active Duty Force Size, 1975–2007

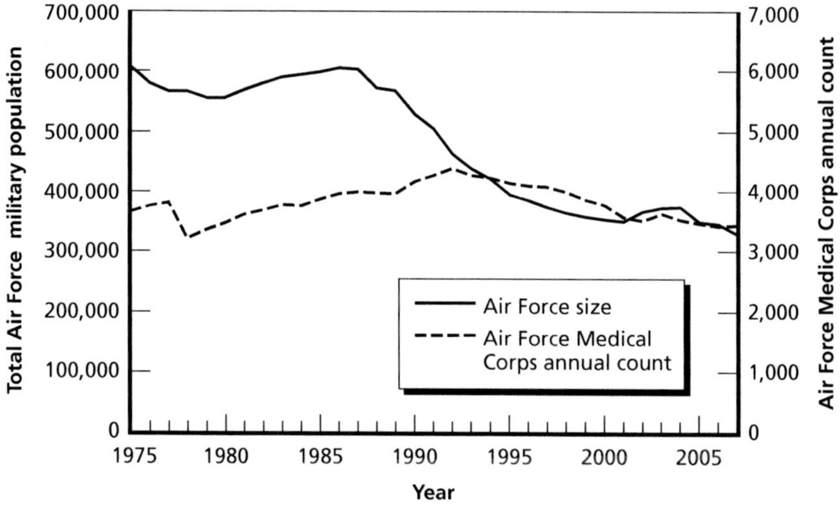

RAND *MG866-2.2*

females and minorities into both the civilian physician labor market and into the Air Force Officer Corps more broadly. In 2007, one-third of all physicians entering the Air Force were female, up from fewer than one-tenth of physicians entering the Medical Corps at the beginning of the 1980s. The annual percentage of women entering the Medical Corps is shown in Figure 2.3, along with data on the percentage of female Air Force officers in those years and the percentage of women graduating from medical school.[7] As Figure 2.3 shows, the percentage

[7] Data on women medical school graduates comes from the DHHS, undated, Table 207, First-Year Enrollments in Schools of Allopathic Medicine By Race and Ethnicity, Academic Years: 1975–76 to 2001–2002. Data on the racial/ethnic composition of medical school graduates can be found in American Association of Medical Colleges, *AAMC Data Book: Statistical Information Related to Medical Education,* Paul Jolly and Dorothea Hudley, eds., Washington, D.C.: American Association of Medical Colleges, 1994. A more recent data extract was provided by Collins Mikesell, a senior analyst at the AAMC. Annual data on gender and race in the Air Force come from data extracts from the U.S. Air Force Personnel Center, Air Force Personnel Statistics, Web page, 2009.

Figure 2.3
Female Graduates of U.S. Medical Schools, Entry of Women into the Medical Corps, and Women in the Air Force Officer Corps, 1975–2007

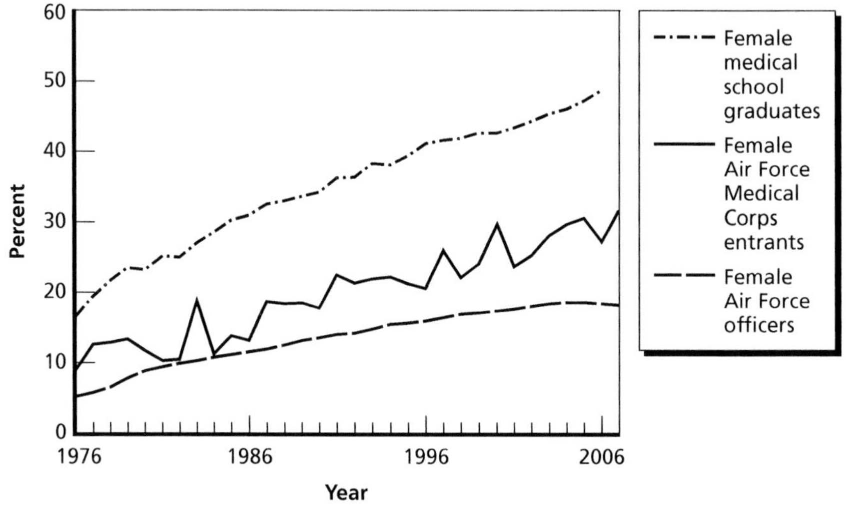

RAND *MG866-2.3*

of women in all three populations has trended up.[8] The percentage of women entering the Medical Corps has consistently been higher than the percentage of women in the Officer Corps as a whole (the better comparison would be with women *entering* the Officer Corps, but we do not have such data) but less than the percentage of female medical school graduates.

In most years, Asian Americans appear to have been the most heavily represented minority group in the Medical Corps. Because Asian Americans were classified in different ways before and after 1993 (for example, some were classified racially as "White" or "Other" and ethnically "Asian" prior to the 1990s), it is difficult to determine precisely how many Asian Americans were in the Medical Corps over time. Across all years, the proportion appears to have fluctuated between

---

[8] To quantify the growth in the share of women in entering cohorts, we subtracted the natural log of the percentage of women in the first year (FY 1976) from the natural log of the percentage of women in the second year (FY 1977), and so forth for each successive year. On average, there has been roughly a 4 percent annual rate of increase in the share of women in Medical Corps entering cohorts.

2 percent and 12 percent of all entrants, averaging roughly 5 percent. There is a discernible pattern of growth in the late 1990s. This corresponds to a time when Asians grew as a proportion of U.S. medical graduates. Annualized rates of growth for Asian medical graduates approached 10 percent during this time. Asians appear to have been a relatively small share of the Air Force Officer Corps in most years (although again, the proportion is sensitive to changing ethnic/racial categorization methodologies).

The proportion of other minorities entering the Medical Corps remained roughly constant during the study period. African-Americans, Hispanics, and Native Americans collectively made up around 3.5 percent of Medical Corps entrants in most years (rates fluctuated from year to year). These minority groups did not experience very high growth in their share of U.S. medical graduates. Underrepresented minorities appear to have made much greater headway entering the Air Force Officer Corps. These groups collectively accounted for more than 10 percent of all Air Force officers during the 1980s and 1990s.

In addition to accession source, gender, and race, our data allow us to examine the specialties of entering physicians. The specialty field of Air Force physicians significantly affected their career prospects, both inside and outside of the Air Force. As shown in Appendix B, both Incentive Special Pay and MSP were affected by a physician's specialty area. Specialty could also have affected the prestige of a physician, both in the military and in the civilian sector.[9]

Within the Medical Corps, we find not only an array of specialty areas but also different levels of training. To take two extremes, a general practice physician (AFSC 44GX)[10] could be qualified to practice medicine after completing a one-year post-graduate internship, whereas

---

[9] Paul Starr, in *The Social Transformation of American Medicine*, New York: Basic Books, 1982, notes that the rising prestige of board-certified specialties over general practitioners in civilian medicine was reinforced by the promotion boards in the U.S. military during World War II. Starr argues that this resulted in increased prestige for board-certified specialties within the military thereafter.

[10] Here we use the AFSC system that went into effect after 1993. A general practice physician in the pre-1993 system would have been a 932X, a neurosurgeon would have been a 941XF.

a neurosurgeon (AFSC 45SXF) would typically complete six years of residency (including general surgery training), and might have also pursued a fellowship in a neurosurgical subfield. The most common training path in internal medicine specialties was to pursue four years of residency training. Those in surgical specialties (including obstetrics and orthopedics) sometimes completed longer residencies and were more likely to pursue fellowships. For a few fields, such as aerospace medicine, emergency medicine, and general medicine, residencies could be completed in an internship year or a two-year program. We classify entrants based on their primary Air Force specialty code (PAFSC).[11] Some classification codes may have been used interchangeably. For example from 1980 to 1984, physicians who were formerly classified as general medical officers were reclassified as family physicians.

Changes in classification practice notwithstanding, the data suggest that many physicians, especially in general medicine, retrained and upgraded their skills while in the Medical Corps. Table 2.1 provides some sense of the migration between different specialties. The rows display the PAFSC of the 10,883 physicians entering the Air Force from 1978 to 2000; the columns display the physician's PAFSC upon leaving the Air Force (or if the physician has not yet left the Air Force, his or her specialty field in 2007). Each cell in the matrix shows the percentage of entrants in the row category who finished their careers in the column category. The "other" category includes several different smaller specialties including dermatology, radiology, and pathology.

Not surprisingly, it was most common for physicians to finish their careers in the same specialty category in which they started (the bold-faced diagonal cells). However, for many specialties, approximately one-third or more of entrants finished their careers with different specialty categories. Some of the most common code changes we observe are out of general practice and into aerospace medicine (18.9 percent), family medicine (14.6 percent),[12] and "other" (21.3 per-

---

[11] In several cases, the entrant came in with the PAFSC of a student, and the duty Air Force specialty code (DAFSC) of a physician in residency training. In these cases, we relied on the DAFSC to determine specialty.

[12] This is likely due to the change in classification practice mentioned previously.

cent). Aside from general practice, specialties that transferred large percentages of entrants into "other" included aerospace medicine (15.5 percent), surgery (13.2 percent), internal medicine (11.1 percent), and family medicine (10.6 percent). Like general medicine, family medicine physicians also transferred into aerospace medicine (10.1 percent of all family medicine entrants). These trends suggest that physicians had the opportunity to advance beyond general medicine into higher-trained specialties while in the Medical Corps. Although comparison is difficult, changing specialties may not be as common in the civilian labor market.[13]

Medical Corps Retention

We next turn to trends in retention and examine how retention has varied by physician characteristics and across time.

One of the potential challenges in analyzing retention is that we risk censoring physicians with longer careers, especially those in more recent cohorts. For example, over half of the physicians who entered in 2002 were still in the Medical Corps in 2007, and many will not complete their minimum service obligations until 2010 and after. We therefore restrict the data analysis in two ways. To ensure that we observe most physicians up to the point of their minimum obligation, we need at least eight years of data (the amount of time from entry into a four-year military residency program to the completion of the minimum service obligation four years after the completion of the residency). For shorter-term outcomes, we focus on entering cohorts from 2000 and before. More than two-thirds of physicians entering between 1978 and

---

[13] The best estimates of switching in the civilian sector come from Nicholas A. Christakis, Jerry A. Jacobs, and Carla M. Messikomer, "Changes in Self-Definition from Specialist to Generalist in a National Sample of Physicians," *Annals of Internal Medicine*, Vol. 121, No. 9, 1994. The authors estimated switching between general and specialized medicine using self-reports from a population sample in the American Medical Association Masterfile from 1982 to 1986. They found that 6.2 percent of generalists switched to a specialty field, and 2.2 percent of the specialists became generalists. Our methodology and time window are somewhat different, so a direct comparison with these estimates is not possible.

Table 2.1
1978–2000 Medical Corps Entrants, by Finishing Specialty (%)

	Final Specialty					
Entering Specialty	Aerospace Medicine	Anesthesiology	Emergency Services	Family Medicine	General Practice	Internal Medicine
Aerospace Medicine	**67.44**	1.49	2.04	3.66	1.09	1.63
Anesthesiology	0.29	**97.94**	0.00	0.59	0.00	0.00
Emergency Services	3.91	0.00	**86.59**	1.40	2.51	0.28
Family Medicine	10.14	0.70	1.66	**68.89**	4.33	0.70
General Practice	18.87	3.55	6.95	14.61	**25.39**	1.28
Internal Medicine	4.59	2.09	1.19	0.60	1.19	**78.43**
OB/Gyn	1.47	0.13	0.27	0.27	0.67	0.27
Orthopedics	0.66	0.00	0.00	0.33	0.00	0.00
Other	2.15	0.09	0.09	0.34	0.34	0.60
Pediatrics	2.06	0.43	0.11	0.43	0.76	0.22
Psychiatry	4.56	0.00	0.76	2.03	1.27	0.25
Surgery	8.26	1.76	2.25	1.04	1.60	0.24
Grand total	10.40	4.11	4.29	16.14	3.27	12.58

Table 2.1—continued

	Final Specialty					
Entering Specialty	OB/Gyn	Orthopedics	Other	Pediatrics	Psychiatry	Surgery
Aerospace Medicine	0.41	4.07	15.47	0.41	0.68	1.63
Anesthesiology	0.00	0.00	0.29	0.00	0.29	0.59
Emergency Services	0.00	0.28	4.47	0.28	0.00	0.28
Family Medicine	0.70	1.31	10.57	0.31	0.48	0.22
General Practice	1.42	3.12	21.28	2.13	1.13	0.28
Internal Medicine	0.06	0.12	11.08	0.12	0.12	0.42
OB/Gyn	**94.24**	0.13	2.41	0.00	0.00	0.13
Orthopedics	0.33	**97.70**	0.33	0.00	0.33	0.33
Other	0.09	0.26	**95.69**	0.17	0.09	0.09
Pediatrics	0.00	0.00	9.86	**85.92**	0.22	0.00
Psychiatry	0.00	0.00	4.56	0.25	**85.82**	0.51
Surgery	0.08	6.98	13.23	0.00	0.08	**64.47**
Grand total	6.76	4.36	19.42	7.57	3.41	7.70

NOTE: OB/Gyn = obstetrics and gynecology.

2000 had left the Medical Corps by the end of their eighth year. To observe longer-career outcomes, such as the first eligibility for military retirement pensions at 20 years of military service, we focus on entering cohorts from 1978 to 1988. A few physicians stay in their careers beyond 20 years, after which they typically advance into the senior leadership of the Medical Corps.

Not surprisingly, the two factors that were most strongly associated with retention were accession source and, for HPSP entrants, whether the physician completed a residency in the military. Table 2.2 summarizes the tenure length (time spent as a physician) in the Medical Corps for physicians who entered from 1978 to 1988. For all groups, there was substantial variation in tenure length. The most extreme variation was among direct accessions, the most heterogeneous group with the lowest average initial service commitments. While almost 13 percent of direct accessions left in the first two years, an even higher percentage stayed for 20 years or longer. (Or, more formally, we saw them in at least 20 annual inventories so we assume they served at least

Table 2.2
Medical Corps Tenure Length, by Accession Source and Residency, 1978–1988 Entrants

Accession Source	Number (% of Total)	Mean Tenure (Standard Dev.)	Modal Tenure	20-Year+ Careers (% of accession source)
HPSP (military residency)	1,902 (37.54)	9.57 (5.54)	7	243 (12.78)
HPSP (civilian residency)[a]	1,202 (23.72)	5.26 (4.15)	4	54 (4.49)
FAP	1 (0.02)	9.00 (N/A)	9	0 (0.00)
USUHS	302 (5.96)	16.31 (5.29)	20	131 (43.38)
Direct accessions	1,291 (25.48)	8.15 (7.00)	3	188 (14.56)
Other accession sources[b]	368 (7.26)	8.73 (6.01)	4	27 (7.34)
Total (all accessions)	5,066 (100.00)	8.53 (6.24)	4	643 (12.69)

[a] Some physicians did not complete any residency.

[b] Interservice transfers, ROTC, etc.

the 20 years required for military pension eligibility.) For all HPSP entrants, the modal tenure length corresponded to minimum service commitment. However, fewer HPSP entrants who served a military residency left after the end of the minimum commitment and they also experienced slower attrition over time than HPSP entrants who served civilian residencies. HPSP entrants who participated in a military residency were almost three times more likely to stay for at least 20 years than HPSP entrants who had not. By far the group with the highest 20-year retention was USUHS graduates. Along with carrying the longest service obligations, USUHS graduates also were, presumably, a population with a much greater taste for military service. As noted in Figure 1.3, USUHS accessions are also more likely to have had prior non–Medical Corps active Air Force experience.

We further stratified accession groups and examined whether retention varied by race, gender, and entering medical specialty area. We show results for the largest accession category, HPSP entrants, in Table 2.3 (military residencies) and Table 2.4 (civilian residencies). We find that African Americans, Native Americans, and Hispanics had longer retention in the Air Force than white non-Hispanics for both HPSP groups. Asians tended to have a retention pattern that was more similar to that of white non-Hispanics in both HPSP groups.

The racial differences in tenure were most marked for HPSP civilian residents: Hispanics, for example, served on average three years longer than did white non-Hispanics. There was no strong evidence of differences in retention by gender.

Retention by entering specialty was more complicated. Retention is measured in years of Air Force service as a physician, not years in the physician's entering specialty. In the military residency group, surgeons had the longest observed retention of any specialty (11.5 years), but, as noted, surgical specialties carry residencies of seven years or longer, and surgeons may have also taken time from their Air Force practice to pursue fellowships. This is why surgeons ranked lower in retention in the civilian resident group.

For the military resident group, the average tenure is also skewed by residency length for the specialties with shorter residencies, such as

Table 2.3
Tenure of HPSP Military Resident Entrants, by Race, Gender, and Entering Specialty, 1978–1988

Characteristic	Number (% of Total)	Mean Tenure (Standard Dev.)	Modal Tenure	20-Year+ Careers (% of Accession Source)
Race				
White non-Hispanic	1,811 (95.21)	9.53 (5.52)	7	229 (12.64)
African American and Native American	47 (2.47)	10.59 (6.13)	11	7 (14.89)
Hispanic	20 (1.05)	10.9 (5.81)	10	4 (20.00)
Asian American	24 (1.26)	8.96 (4.87)	10	2 (8.33)
Gender				
Male	1,648 (86.65)	9.62 (5.54)	7	208 (12.62)
Female	254 (13.35)	9.20 (5.55)	7	34 (13.43)
Specialty				
Aerospace Medicine	245 (12.88)	8.36 (6.19)	4	31 (12.65)
Emergency Services	12 (.63)	5.58 (3.26)	3	0 (0.00)
Anesthesiology	39 (2.05)	8.10 (3.55)	7	2 (5.13)
General Practice	49 (2.58)	9.41 (6.42)	5	8 (16.33)
Family Medicine	504 (26.50)	9.27 (6.17)	7	75 (14.88)
Internal Medicine	354 (18.61)	9.96 (4.64)	9	36 (10.17)
OB/Gyn	114 (5.99)	8.33 (3.09)	8	2 (1.75)
Orthopedics	6 (.32)	4.67 (3.14)	3	0 (0.00)
Surgery	240 (12.62)	11.49 (5.12)	9	38 (15.83)
Pediatrics	187 (9.88)	10.85 (6.26)	7	40 (21.39)
Psychiatry	104 (5.47)	8.66 (3.91)	8	5 (4.81)
Other	47 (2.47)	8.91 (4.71)	8	5 (10.64)
Total	1,902 (100)	9.57 (5.54)	7	242 (12.73)

Table 2.4
Tenure of HPSP Civilian Resident Entrants, by Race, Gender, and Entering Specialty, 1978–1988

Characteristic	Number (% of Total)	Mean Tenure (Standard Dev.)	Modal Tenure	20-Year+ Careers (% of Accession Source)
Race				
White non-Hispanic	1,115 (92.76)	5.12 (3.93)	4	43 (3.86)
African American and Native American	46 (3.82)	7.19 (6.36)	4	6 (13.04)
Hispanic	28 (2.32)	8.25 (6.59)	4	5 (21.43)
Asian American	13 (1.08)	4.77 (1.96)	4	0 (0.00)
Gender				
Male	1,042 (86.69)	5.04 (4.20)	4	47 (4.51)
Female	160 (13.31)	5.30 (3.82)	4	7 (4.38)
Specialty				
Aerospace Medicine	9 (.75)	7.11 (4.04)	4	0 (0.00)
Emergency Services	33 (2.75)	4.37 (2.49)	4	0 (0.00)
Anesthesiology	59 (4.91)	3.80 (5.13)	4	0 (0.00)
General Practice	115 (27.95)	6.83 (5.13)	4	8 (6.96)
Family Medicine	336 (27.95)	5.78 (5.05)	4	23 (6.85)
Internal Medicine	165 (13.73)	5.62 (4.00)	4	8 (4.85)
OB/Gyn	89 (7.40)	4.47 (3.46)	4	3 (3.37)
Orthopedics	58 (5.83)	4.17 (2.79)	4	1 (1.72)
Surgery	61 (5.07)	4.85 (3.49)	4	2 (3.28)
Pediatrics	94 (7.82)	5.41 (4.72)	4	7 (7.45)
Psychiatry	14 (1.16)	4.14 (2.03)	4	0 (0.00)
Other	169 (14.06)	4.36 (2.35)	4	2 (1.18)
Total (All HPSP civilian residents)	1,202 (100)	5.26 (4.15)	4	54 (4.49)

aerospace medicine and emergency medicine. Looking at the civilian residency group, we see that, once the results are not distorted by residency length, those groups tend to have longer average tenure. For the civilian residency group, physicians in internal and general medicine specialties tended to stay longer than those in the surgical specialties (including anesthesiology, obstetrics, and orthopedics).

In both groups, the entering specialty with the highest 20-year retention rate was pediatricians. Long-term retention of pediatricians has not been a major challenge for the Air Force; they were not offered four-year Special Pay in FY08. Some caution is appropriate when interpreting these results. First, because many of the specialty groups had fewer than 50 physicians entering during the study period, chance variation, rather than consistent differences in retention behavior, may have driven some of the observed differences. Second, we look here only at physicians' entering AFSC. As noted in Table 2.1, it was not uncommon for physicians to change specialties during their Air Force careers. Finally, these data only provide a snapshot of entering cohorts through 1988.

We did not find any strong evidence that retention has changed consistently over time. Examining entering cohorts from 1978 to 2000, stratified by mode of accession and residency status, we find that short-term retention (retention within the first seven years of entrance) for HPSP entrants in military residencies hovered around 55 percent of all entrants in most entering cohorts; for HPSP entrants with civilian residencies, the proportion was generally 5–15 percent. Short-term retention was more variable for other accession groups, but this result is skewed by the relatively small number of entrants in many years. Long-term retention (20 years or longer) was generally 12–18 percent for HPSP entrants in military residencies and around 3–8 percent for HPSP entrants with civilian residencies. Again, the small number of entrants in many years prevents us from comparing 20-year retention over time within those accession groups.

Medical Corps Promotion

Promotions in the Medical Corps are determined by the Air Force promotion board. These promotions tend to follow a well-ordered timeline. Most physicians enter the Medical Corps at the rank of captain (O-3). Physicians are placed on a promotion list in their order of entry, which then affects their order of consideration for promotions. Physicians and dentists are exempt from Defense Officer Personnel Management Act (DOPMA) constraints on the number of majors, lieutenant colonels, and colonels allowed on active duty in the Air Force.[14]

A captain is typically considered for a promotion to major (O-4) by the first promotion board that meets after his or her sixth year of credited service. The promotion from captain to major is generally not competitive; it is awarded to all qualified physicians. The next promotion from major to lieutenant colonel (O-5) generally takes place an additional six years after the promotion to major. This promotion is more competitive than the promotion to major, although the promotion rate is high for eligible physicians. Many physicians, however, leave the Medical Corps before consideration for promotion to lieutenant colonel. The promotion from lieutenant colonel to colonel is typically considered by the promotion board six years after the promotion to lieutenant colonel. This is a competitive promotion that some eligible lieutenant colonel physicians do not receive.

At every promotion point, it is possible for a physician to be promoted in fewer than six years. Physicians could be awarded constructive credit for civilian experience. For example, an HPSP physician who served a four-year residency at a civilian medical center would generally be awarded four years of constructive credit upon entering the Medical Corps. Hence, upon entrance, such a physician would be only two years away from being considered for promotion to major. Similarly, direct accessions with civilian experience could be awarded constructive credit for that experience, resulting in a higher grade upon entrance and/or a shorter time to the first promotion. Likewise,

---

[14] See 10 U.S.C. 523b.

pre–Medical Corps military service can result in faster promotion as a physician.

Another possibility, although quite rare, is that a physician could be awarded a "below the zone" promotion, a promotion that takes place in less than six years. Below-the-zone promotions are reserved for officers who have distinguished themselves, demonstrating exceptional leadership qualities or the potential to become a general officer someday.

Because our data do not allow us to determine when an officer was first considered for promotion, we cannot infer whether an early promotion was due to constructive credit or was below the zone. Furthermore, because physicians enter the Medical Corps on a rolling basis during a fiscal year, physicians in a given entering cohort may be up for their first promotions in different fiscal years (especially if a promotion board only meets once in a year).

Direct accessions, especially in the 1970s and early 1980s, were relatively more likely to enter the Medical Corps at the grade of major or higher than other accessions. As mentioned above, entrants at the mid-career level during this period were credited with years of service reflecting their experience in the civilian sector. Of the 1,291 direct accessions from 1978 to 1988, 647 (50 percent) entered as captain, 462 (36 percent) entered at major, and 182 (14 percent) entered at lieutenant colonel. By comparison, of the remaining 3,775 entrants into the Medical Corps between 1978 and 1988 who were not direct accessions, 3,614 (96 percent) entered at captain, 128 entered at major (3 percent), and 33 entered at lieutenant colonel (1 percent).

In cases in which we observed promotions taking place in less than six years, we found evidence that accession source correlated with accelerated promotion. USUHS graduates tended to experience faster promotion both from O-4 to O-5 and from O-5 to O-6 than did HPSP entrants who went through civilian residencies. HPSP entrants from military residencies also experienced faster promotion than their counterparts who completed civilian residencies. This finding again might reflect a higher degree of taste for military service among those who completed military residencies (and hence more leadership or commitment to military service). Direct accessions appeared to experience higher rates of promotion under six years. However, this population was also more likely to receive credited years of service, so the speed of promotion may have reflected not only merit, but also credit for civilian experience of this group. Figures 2.4 and 2.5 illustrate the speed of promotion from O-4 to O-5 and from O-5 to O-6.

There is likely a dynamic interaction between retention and promotion: Part of a physician's decision to stay in the military may have been based on the physician's belief that he or she would be promoted to a higher grade in a certain span of time. Physicians who believed that promotion was unlikely may have self-selected themselves out or may have been encouraged to leave the service. We especially find evidence of this at higher grades, a point at which physicians who have advanced to the position of colonel generally take on additional teaching, mentorship, and leadership responsibilities. Lieutenant colonels who stayed for 20 years or longer likely judged that they would not be promoted after their twentieth year, and began planning a second

Figure 2.4
Percentage of Medical Corps Majors Promoted to Lieutenant Colonel in Less Than Six Years, Six Years, or More Than Six Years, by Accession Source, 1978–1988

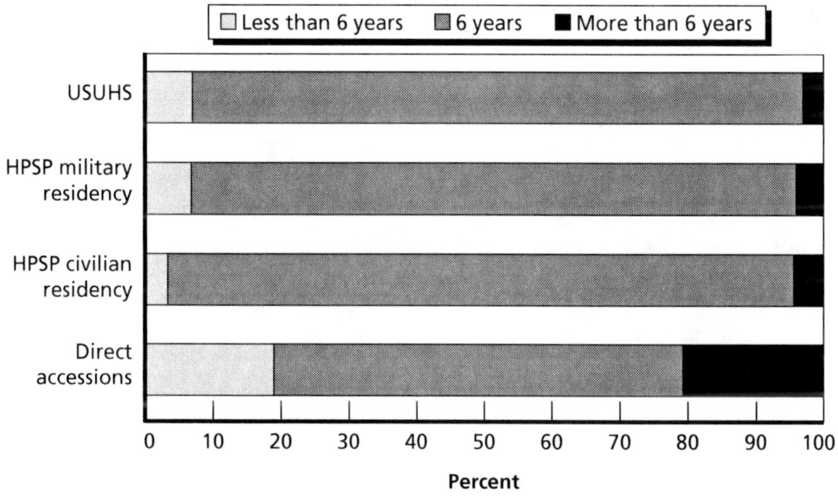

RAND *MG866-2.4*

Figure 2.5
Percentage of Medical Corps Lieutenant Colonels Promoted to Colonel in Less Than Six Years, Six Years, or More Than Six Years, by Accession Source, 1978–1988

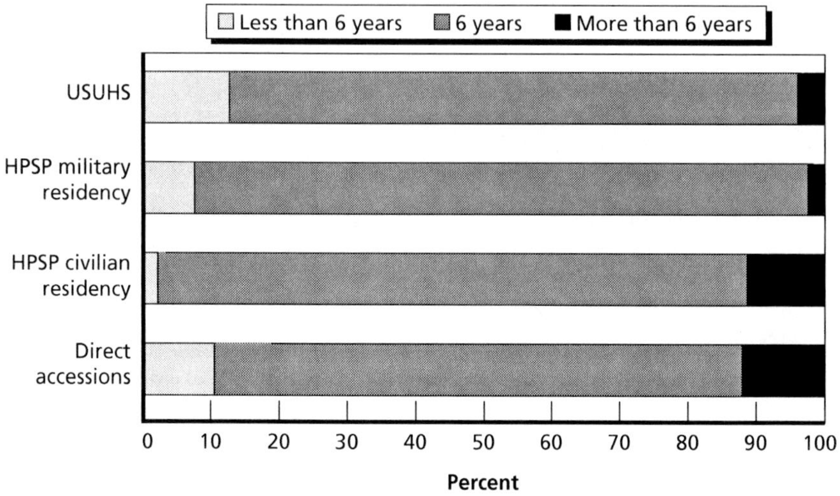

RAND *MG866-2.5*

career in the civilian sector after they became eligible for a military pension. As Figure 2.6 illustrates, lieutenant colonels are much more likely to leave in their twentieth year than are colonels.

Another explanation for the result shown in Figure 2.6 is the High-3 pension system that applied to most of the physicians analyzed.[15] A newly promoted colonel has incentive to stay in the Air Force for three years at that rank so he or she receives the full colonel's pension. By contrast, a physician who is a lieutenant colonel at Year 20 has doubtlessly qualified for the full lieutenant colonel pension and is at least three years away from receiving a full colonel pension (even if promotion to colonel were imminent). So a lieutenant colonel has less incremental financial incentive to stay in the Air Force past 20 years than a newly promoted colonel does.

---

[15] See Office of the Under Secretary of Defense for Personnel and Readiness, "High-3 Year Average Retirement System," Web page, no date, for more information about the High-3 pension system.

Figure 2.6
Percentage of Physicians Retiring in Year, Conditional on Staying for More Than 19 Years, 1978–1988 Entering Cohorts

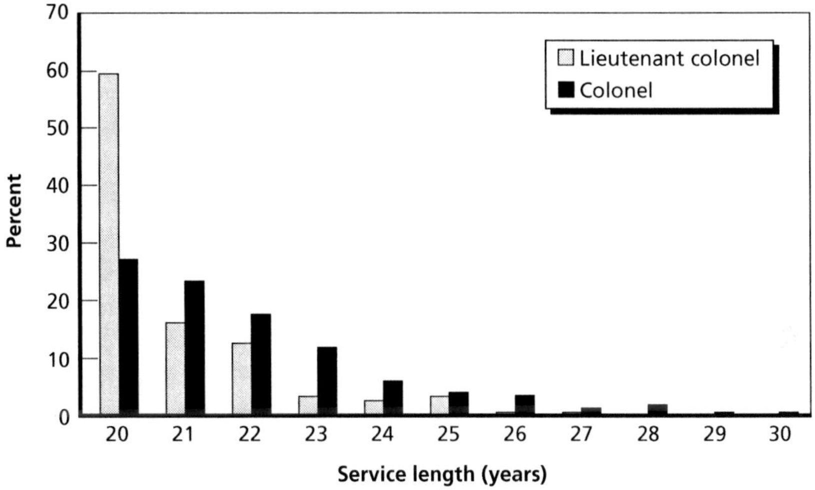

RAND *MG866-2.6*

We did not find any evidence strongly suggesting that promotion differed by gender or race. After controlling for residency status in the entry year, the time to promotion between white non-Hispanic and African American (the largest minority group) physicians were quite similar. However, we are limited in testing this hypothesis because of the relatively small sample sizes of the different groups. For example, we could not further stratify the groups and test for differences by specific accession sources. This was especially true for the promotion from lieutenant colonel to colonel—only 17 African Americans who entered at the rank of captain attained the rank of colonel or higher from the 1978–1988 entering cohorts.

In the next chapter, we focus on the issue of MSP and physicians' tendencies to accept it.

CHAPTER THREE
Physician Cohort Analysis

Having provided an overview of Air Force physician accession, retention, and promotion, we next examine recent entering cohorts to study physicians' predilection to accept MSP.

Members of the entering cohorts displayed in Figure 1.2 have in common that they became Air Force physicians in the same fiscal year. There were, for example, 541 physicians who entered the Air Force Medical Corps in FY89 (i.e., the first time we saw them as physicians in the Air Force was in the September 30, 1989, military personnel inventory).

While members of an entering cohort share their first year of service as Air Force physicians, intracohort heterogeneity remains considerable. In particular, some members of an entering cohort have already completed civilian residency programs (either as deferred HPSP accessions or through the FAP); others are just starting military residency programs. Additionally, an entering cohort is made up of physicians from a range of medical specialties. Figure 3.1 estimates the number of physicians who entered Air Force service with and without residency training already completed[1] between 1989 and 2007.[2]

---

[1] The annual military personnel inventories do not explicitly indicate whether a physician has completed residency training. Instead, we used each entering physician's Air Force specialty code in conjunction with the graduate professional education variable to estimate each physician's entering status. Our methodology is discussed in Appendix A.

[2] The 1989 entering cohort is the earliest cohort we analyze in this chapter. The Air Force adopted its current MSP program in 1990; the first year for which we have a complete tabulation of those pay levels was 1992. Hence, we restricted our analysis to entering cohorts

Figure 3.1
Physicians Entering Air Force Service With and Without Completed Civilian Residencies

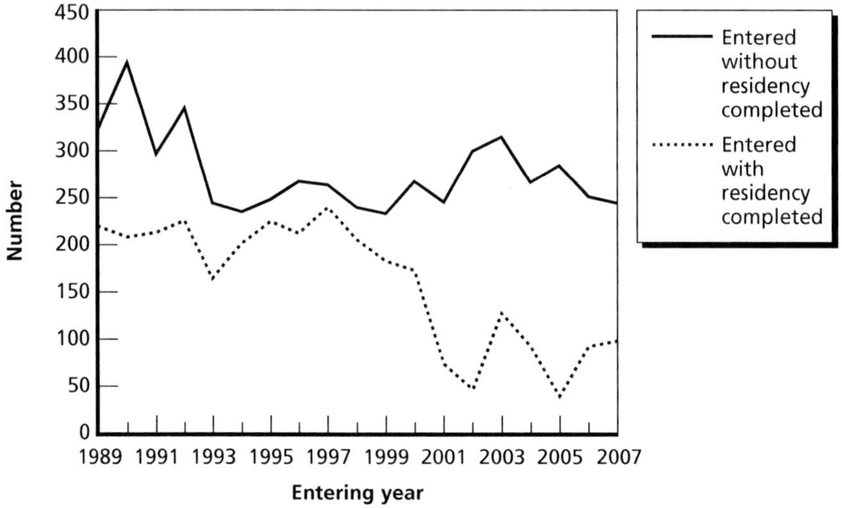

RAND *MG866-3.1*

While the number of entering physicians has drifted downward, the number of physicians entering without a completed residency (i.e., entering into a military residency program) has been fairly static.

It appears that the process works as follows: Each year, the Air Force has a varying number of new HPSP and USUHS medical school graduates. The Air Force inducts enough of these new graduates to fill the slots it has in military residency programs. Almost all USUHS graduates, it appears, enter military residency programs. By contrast, some HPSP physicians serve military residencies while others perform civilian residencies. The default is for an HPSP physician to serve a military residency; a physician needs a deferment from the Air Force to have a residency at a civilian medical center. As total accessions have declined (see Figure 1.2), the number of physicians entering with resi-

---

whose members were almost certainly exposed to the current MSP program. As shown in Figure 3.2, few members of the 1989 entering cohort left Air Force service before the beginning of FY92.

dency training at a civilian medical center has declined disproportionately, as shown in Figure 3.1.

Physicians who enter Air Force service having already completed a civilian residency are typically just three or four years away from being eligible to leave the Air Force (having, after three or four years, fulfilled their HPSP or FAP service obligation). By contrast, physicians whose first service is as a military resident are many more years away from fulfilling their service obligation, since years in a military residency do not count toward HPSP or USUHS obligation fulfillment.[3]

Figure 3.2 uses 1989 physician cohort data to show the sharp differences in retention behavior that can occur between those physicians who enter the Air Force having completed a civilian residency and those who enter the Air Force serving a military residency. "1989 entered with residency completed" physicians entered the Air

Figure 3.2
Retention Rates of FY89 Cohort Physicians Who Completed Civilian Residencies Versus Physicians Who Had Not

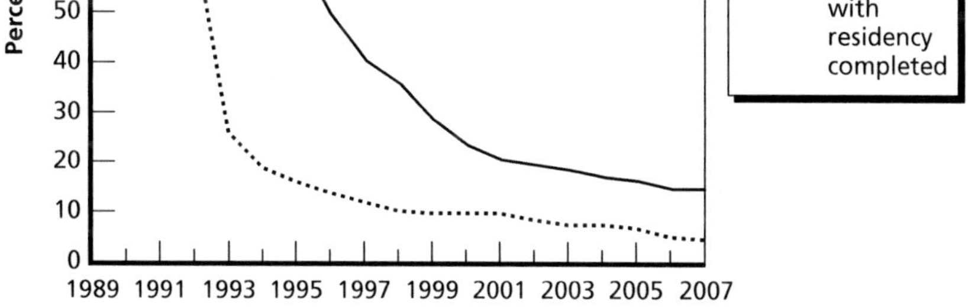

RAND *MG866-3.2*

[3] Logically, a physician in a military residency program should not have an FAP obligation since FAP is paid to civilian physicians in residency training.

Force having already completed a civilian residency. "1989 entered without residency completed" physicians entered the Air Force having not yet completed a residency; typically, they entered into military residency programs. The "1989 entered with residency completed" population departed Air Force service at a much faster rate.

Almost all of the physicians who entered with their residency completed became eligible to leave the Air Force in three or four years when their HPSP or FAP obligations were fulfilled. By contrast, physicians who entered without their residency completed had considerable variance as to when they completed residency training and, hence, when they were first eligible to leave the Air Force.

The sharp differences in Figure 3.2 are not necessarily caused by civilian versus military residency programs per se. The data show almost all USUHS graduates are funneled into military residency programs. So the marked difference shown in Figure 3.2 at least in part reflects differences in taste for military service between those in civilian and military residency programs. It seems reasonable to suppose, for instance, that an individual with a preference for military service would be inclined to attend USUHS for medical school rather than a civilian institution. Physicians with a high taste for military service, such as USUHS graduates, are disproportionately found in the "1989 entered without residency completed" population.[4]

The issue of civilian versus military residencies is of direct interest to this study because of the regulations governing eligibility to receive MSP. According to DoD Financial Management Regulations,[5] a Medical or Dental Corps officer is eligible for MSP if he or she has

- completed appropriate residency training (civilian or military)
- at least eight years of creditable service OR completed any active duty service obligation incurred for medical education and training.

---

4 *Taste for military service*, i.e., how much or how little someone likes being in the military, is an important parameter in Dynamic Retention Model estimation. See Appendix D.

5 See U.S. Department of Defense, *Financial Management Regulation*, *Volume 7A*, Chapter 5, November 2008.

Consider an HPSP-educated physician who enters Air Force service having completed a civilian residency. Once this physician has fulfilled his or her three- or four-year HPSP commitment, he or she is eligible for MSP—or to leave the Air Force altogether. Figure 3.2 shows that most physicians in the FY89 entering cohort who completed civilian residencies (either after having HPSP pay for medical school or who received FAP support during their residencies) chose to leave Air Force service at their first opportunity to do so.

Next consider an HPSP-educated physician who enters Air Force service as a military resident. This physician will likely not complete residency training for three to five years and only after completing training will begin to fulfill the HPSP obligation. For this physician, completion of eight years of creditable service and completion of the HPSP obligation will probably occur in relatively close proximity.

Finally, consider a USUHS-educated physician in a military residency. This physician will almost certainly hit the eight years of creditable service point before he or she pays off the seven-year, postresidency USUHS obligation. This physician could therefore accept MSP prior to fulfillment of his or her USUHS obligation. Few, however, do so: If an officer with a pending initial educational obligation accepts MSP, years are added to the end of his or her commitment one-for-one. Further, if MSP is taken prior to fulfillment of the seven-year, postresidency USUHS obligation, there will be "leftover" years at the back end of the obligation in which the physician would not be eligible for MSP.[6]

By contrast, if a physician takes MSP and then subsequently incurs additional educational obligations (e.g., through further training), the MSP and educational obligations could be fulfilled concur-

---

[6] If a physician believed MSP levels were static or were not going to increase at his or her personal rate of interest, it might be reasonable to take MSP now and leave MSP-free leftover years at the end of his or her career (assuming he or she wanted to stay in the Air Force past expiration of the initial service commitment). However, as discussed in Appendixes B and C, MSP levels have increased sharply in recent years, doubtlessly to the chagrin of any near-retirement physicians with such leftover, MSP-free years.

rently.[7] A physician who anticipates future additional training has an incentive to first fulfill all pending educational obligations (e.g., from USUHS), accept MSP, and then enter into additional training, such as a fellowship. The system gives an incentive to physicians to behave strategically with respect to the timing of MSP acceptance and additional training.

Figure 3.3 shows the years in which we estimate the FY89 entering cohort's physicians first became eligible for MSP. Using AFPC data, we estimated, on a physician-by-physician basis, when individuals first became eligible for MSP; eligibility status is not indicated in the personnel data we received, necessitating our estimation. Our estimation procedure is discussed in Appendix A.

Twenty-eight physicians entered the Air Force in 1989 as fully qualified, direct appointments. They were immediately eligible for

Figure 3.3
Years That FY89 Entering Cohort Physicians Became Eligible for MSP

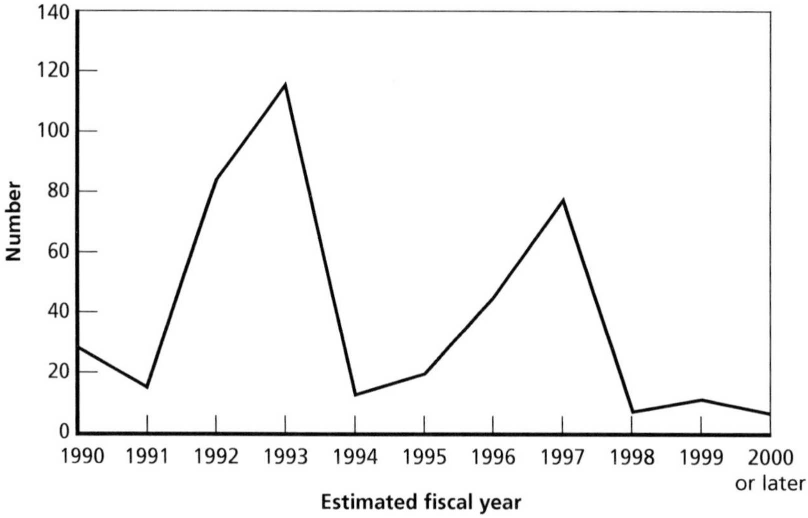

RAND *MG866-3.3*

[7] See U.S. Department of the Air Force, *Active Duty Service Commitments*, Air Force Instruction 36-2107, April 22, 2005.

MSP when that program started in 1990 because they had completed civilian residency training on their own and did not owe the Air Force service due to HPSP, FAP, or USUHS support. These are the physicians shown at "1990" on the x-axis.

A much larger population (the 1992 and 1993 peak) that we call *early eligibles* entered the Air Force in FY89 having completed a civilian residency but owing years of service under HPSP or FAP. Once these individuals paid off their initial service obligation (typically in three or four years—1992 or 1993), they were eligible for MSP or to leave Air Force service altogether.

The second large peak in Figure 3.3 is for physicians who completed military residencies. In 1997, the FY89 cohort physicians hit the eight-years-of-service point, so any physician with a completed residency as of that year became eligible for MSP, irrespective of any yet-unfulfilled educational obligation. We define physicians whose first MSP eligibility occurs in Year 6 (1995 for FY89 entering cohort physicians) or later as *later eligibles*.[8]

There were 95 members of the FY89 entering cohort who left the Air Force prior to becoming eligible to accept MSP. These physicians were general medical officers, emergency services physicians, and aerospace medicine physicians who did not complete MSP-qualifying residency programs.[9]

The distinction between early eligibles (e.g., HPSP and FAP physicians who enter with completed civilian residencies) and later eligibles

---

[8] Other researchers, e.g., Brannman et al. (2003), use the terms "HPSP direct accession" and "HPSP deferred accession" similarly to our later eligibles and early eligibles, respectively. The only minor difference is that we also include FAP accessions (who have completed civilian residencies upon commencement of Air Force service) in the early eligibles category. See Shayne Brannman et al., *Life-Cycle Costs of Selected Uniformed Health Professions (Phase II: The Impact of Constraints and Policies on the Optimal-Mix-of-Accession Model)*, Alexandria, Va.: Center for Naval Analyses, CRM D0007887.A2/Final, April 2003.

[9] We used an algorithm whereby physicians with primary AFSCs 44E3 (emergency services physician), 44G3 (general medical officer), and 48G3 (aerospace medicine physician) were deemed not to be MSP-eligible. Further complicating our analysis, the Air Force switched AFSC systems between 1993 and 1994. The AFSCs for 1993 and earlier versions of these non-MSP eligible were 9396 (emergency services physician), 9326 (general practice physician), and 9356 (aerospace medicine physician).

(physicians who completed military residencies) is an important one. Figure 3.4 illustrates why. About 8 percent of the early eligible physicians in the FY89 cohort (those whom we estimate became MSP-eligible between 1992 and 1994) accepted MSP. (We used payroll data from the Defense Manpower Data Center to ascertain which physicians accepted MSP.[10]) As shown in Figure 3.2, most early eligibles (who, by definition, entered with a civilian residency already completed) left the Air Force at their first opportunity to do so. By contrast, about 33 percent of later eligible physicians in the FY89 entering cohort (those who became MSP-eligible in 1995 and later) accepted MSP.

Figure 3.4
FY89 Entering Cohort Physician MSP Acceptance Rates, by First Year of MSP Eligibility

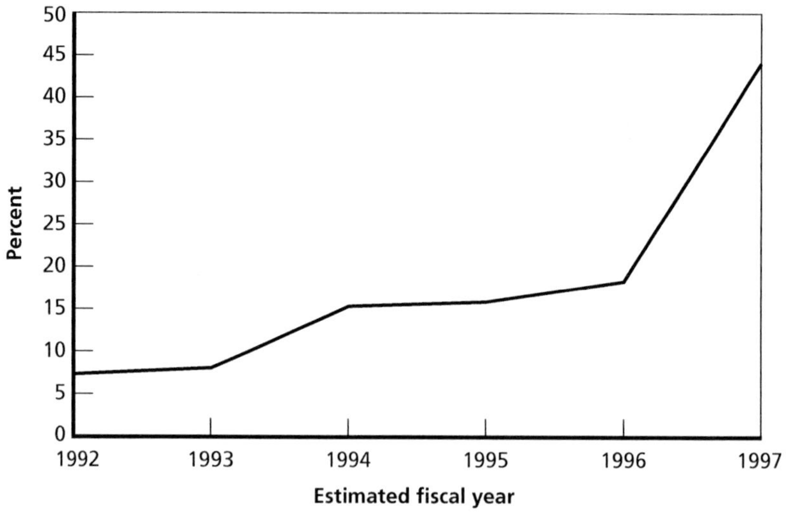

RAND *MG866-3.4*

[10] There is also a "reason code" in the personnel data in which "48" denotes an individual who accepted MSP. Unfortunately, analysis of payroll data indicated that reason code 48 is underreported in the personnel data. So we relied on the DMDC payroll data to tell us which physicians received MSP.

While Figures 3.2–3.4 focus on the FY89 entering cohort, Figure 3.5 shows the early and later eligible MSP acceptance rates for the 1989–2003 cohorts. (A physician is deemed to have accepted MSP if he or she accepted it any time between becoming eligible through and including September 2007.)

In every entering cohort between 1989 and 1998, the MSP acceptance rate was higher for later eligibles (those who performed military residencies) than for early eligibles (those who performed civilian residencies).

There appears to be a downward trend in the MSP acceptance rate for later eligibles. At least for the 1999 and 2000 entering cohorts, this result is probably spurious: 2006 was the first year a later eligible in the FY00 cohort could accept MSP. MSP acceptances often occur a few years after eligibility attainment, e.g., the physician neither leaves the Air Force nor accepts MSP for a few years. We strongly suspect that future data will show an upturn in MSP acceptance rates among later eligibles in more-recent cohorts. Given the medical academic calendar,

Figure 3.5
MSP Acceptance Rates, by Physician Entering Cohort and Eligibility Timing

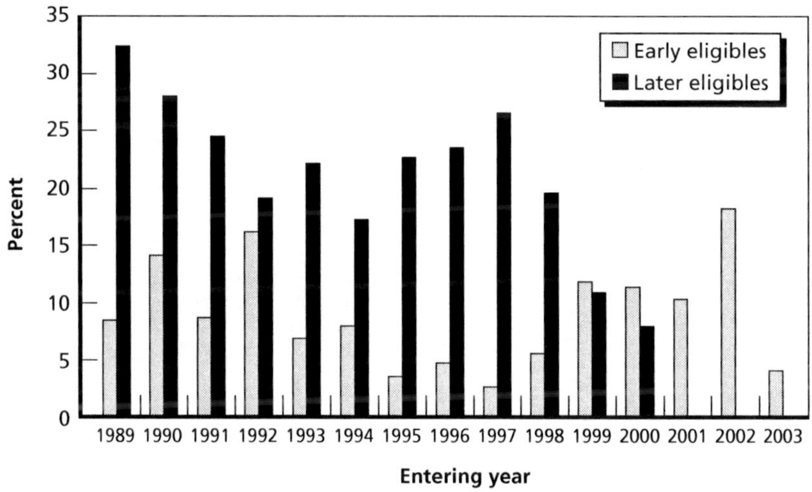

RAND *MG866-3.5*

most physicians start military service in June or July, so later eligible physicians in the 2001 entering cohort would have had only a couple of months to accept MSP by September 30, 2007. According to the payroll data we analyzed, none did. Later eligible physicians in the 2002 entering cohort first became eligible to accept MSP during FY08.

Early eligible MSP acceptance rates appeared to be higher for the early 1990s cohorts than for the mid-1990s cohorts. The early eligibles in the 1995–1998 cohorts seemed highly disinclined to accept MSP. In aggregate, they had a MSP acceptance rate of less than 5 percent. This adverse trend has reversed itself more recently, with early eligibles in the 1999–2002 entering cohorts showing a greater predilection to accept MSP.

Figure 3.6 is a different cut of the same MSP acceptance data, except that it is plotted by estimated first year of eligibility rather than by entering cohort year. We have italicized "Estimated" to underscore the fact we had to estimate, on a physician-by-physician basis, when individuals became eligible to receive MSP. See Appendix A.

Figure 3.6
Physician MSP Acceptance Rates, by First Year of Eligibility and Eligibility Timing

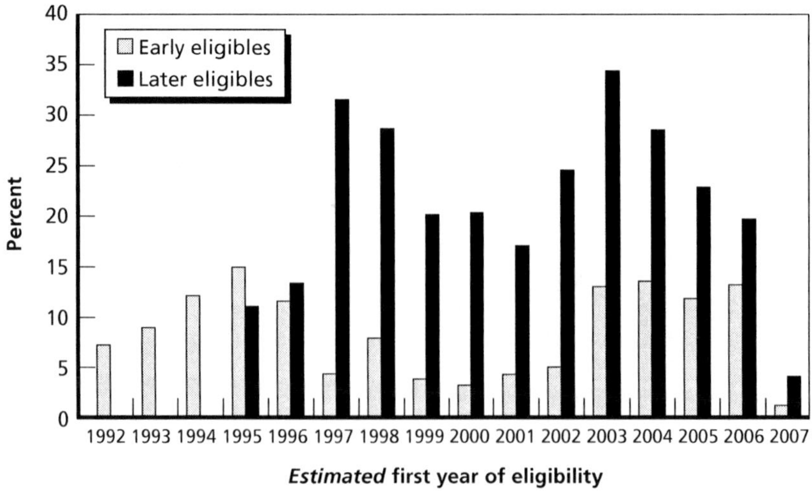

RAND *MG866-3.6*

Like Figure 3.5, Figure 3.6 shows a general tendency for later eligible physicians to be more predisposed to accept MSP. Given that our cohort analysis starts with the FY89 entering cohort, we do not observe any later eligible physicians until 1995. Consistent with Figure 3.5, there is an MSP acceptance trough in the middle of the data, most notably for early eligibles who became MSP-eligible between 1999 and 2002. Given the modal four-year HPSP obligation, the low MSP-acceptance 1995–1998 entering cohorts in Figure 3.5 are largely the same physicians who form the low MSP-acceptance 1999–2002 first-year-of-eligibility cohorts in Figure 3.6.

The 2007 value in Figure 3.6 is artificially depressed; we expect a number of these newly eligible physicians to accept MSP in the next year or two. Physicians who became MSP-eligible during FY07 typically only had a couple of months between becoming eligible and the September 2007 annual snapshot.

As was true in Figure 3.5, there are some grounds for optimism in Figure 3.6: The 2003–2006 first-year-of-eligibility cohorts have greater MSP acceptance rates, both for late and early eligibles, than its predecessor cohorts (most notably 1999–2002).

One explanation for the recent upturn in physician MSP acceptance rates is the increases in MSP levels shown in Appendix B. Appendix C presents a logistic regression analysis of physician MSP acceptance that estimates how increased MSP levels increase MSP acceptance. We believe the upturn in MSP acceptance rates for more recent cohorts has been driven, at least in part, by increases in MSP levels.

In the next chapter we present an overview of Air Force Dental Corps accession, retention, and promotion patterns.

CHAPTER FOUR

Trends in Accession, Retention, and Promotion in the Air Force Dental Corps, 1976–2007

In this chapter, we examine some of the patterns in Air Force dentist accession, retention, and promotion for entering cohorts from 1976 to 2007. The structure of this chapter is very similar to that of Chapter Two, although some of the major trends in the Dental Corps differ from those in the Medical Corps.

As with the previous chapters, the main data resource is the annual military personnel inventories, the latest of which was as of September 30, 2007. In total, the data file contains records for 4,112 dentists whom we observe entering the Air Force Dental Corps between October 1975 and September 2007.[1] For the entering cohorts prior to the 1990s, the longer time series allows us to observe long-term outcomes, such as promotions later in a dentist's career and retention after the dentist becomes eligible for a military pension (after 20 years of service). This longer time series also allows us to examine variation within and across different cohorts, providing a rich picture of changing service patterns over time.

Patterns in Dental Corps Accessions

Direct accessions were the primary Dental Corps accession source during the study period. This accession category consists of dentists who

---

[1] An additional 1,768 dentists who entered prior to October 1, 1975, were omitted from the analysis because an exact entry year could not be determined.

had already completed dental school upon joining the Air Force. Direct accessions received no financial assistance from the Air Force prior to their commencement of services. As Figure 4.1 illustrates, direct accessions made up virtually all of the entrants through the 1980s, and continued to be a high proportion into the mid-1990s. Only in the late 1990s did HPSP graduates begin to overtake direct accessions, a process that had started much earlier in the Medical Corps (see Figure 2.1).

Beginning in 1996, the share of entrants from HPSP grew at a rapid pace. In 1995, fewer than 20 percent of all entrants were HPSP graduates, but by 2000 the HPSP share of entrants had increased to over 80 percent of all Dental Corps entrants. Unlike HPSP graduates in the Medical Corps, very few HPSP graduates in the Dental Corps pursued civilian residencies after completing dental school. More often, dentists either began practicing full-time in the Dental Corps directly out of dental school or received further training in a one-year internship provided by the Air Force. We estimate that about one-third of all entrants from HPSP (and a similar proportion of direct accessions)

Figure 4.1
Changing Accession Sources of Dental Corps Entrants, 1978–2000

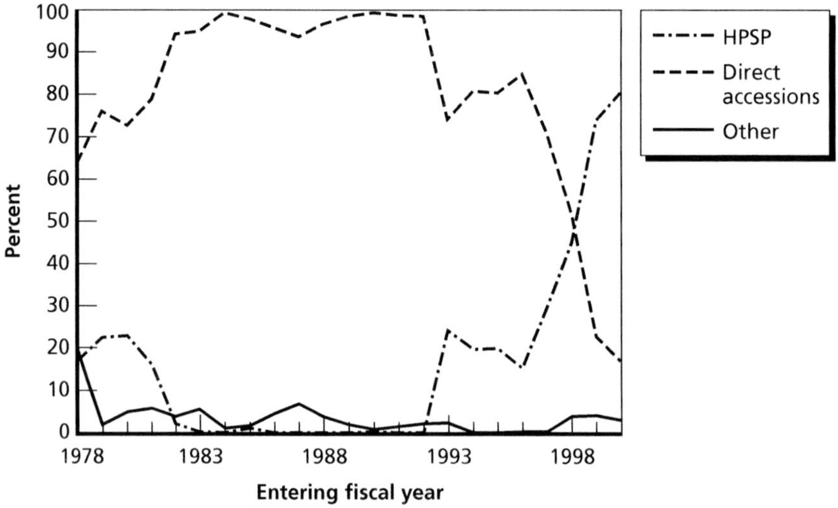

RAND *MG866-4.1*

spent their first year in the Dental Corps in an Air Force-provided one-year training program.

Few dentists enrolled in the FAP program. Indeed, only 14 entrants during the period from 1978 to 2000 accessed through FAP. These 14 entrants are included in the "Other" category in Figure 4.1, along with several other smaller accession sources, such as ROTC and interservice transfers. USUHS is a medical school, not a dental school, so there were no USUHS accessions into the Dental Corps.

As shown in Figure 4.2, the total population of dentists during the study period showed a high correlation with the Air Force population as a whole. Both populations peaked in the mid-1990s and declined quite steeply until around 2000. There was an increase in the Air Force population between 2001 and 2004, followed by a decline between 2004 and 2007; the Air Force Dental Corps declined in size throughout the same period, except for a small increase between 2003 and 2004. The Air Force population declined 61 percent from 1975 to 2007; the Dental Corps declined by 49 percent during the same period.

Figure 4.2
Annual Dental Corps and Air Force Active Duty Force Size, 1975–2007

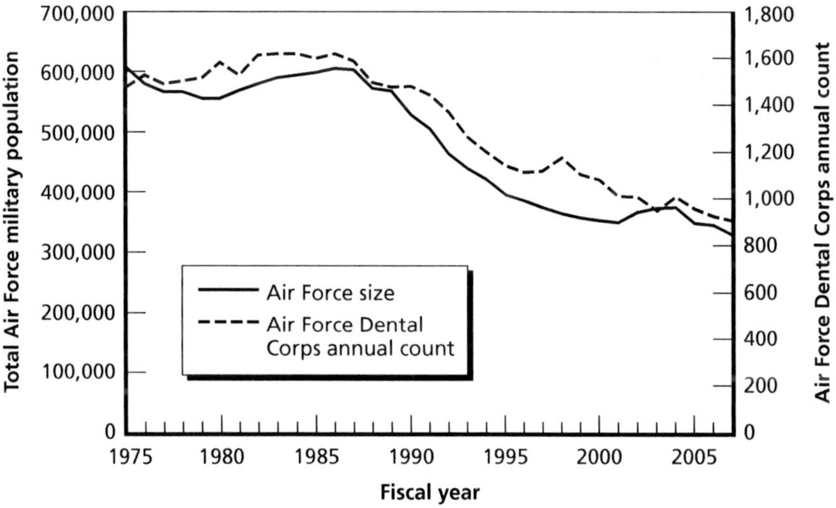

RAND *MG866-4.2*

During the period of these data, dentists' wages in the civilian labor market increased. This increase was partially driven by increasing demand for dentists without an equivalent increase in supply. More people in the population began using dental services regularly while the dentist-to-population ratio began declining around 1995.[2] The relative scarcity of dentists was accompanied by rapidly increasing incomes. From 1982 to 2000, there was a real increase in net income of dentists (subtracting out practice expenses) of over 50 percent.[3] The median wages in the civilian labor market for dentists with such specialties as orthodontics and prosthodontics in 2007 rivaled those of many medical specialties.[4]

As with the Medical Corps, the share of women entering the Dental Corps increased during the study period. From 1978 to 2007, the share of women entering the Dental Corps increased at an annualized rate of 4.6 percent (from under 10 percent in 1978 to about 30 percent in 2007). By comparison, the average annual rate of growth in the share of women in the entire Air Force Officer Corps from 1978 to 2007 was 4.1 percent (from just over 5 percent in 1978 to just under 20 percent in 2007).[5] Comparable data on the share of women graduating from dental school were available only from 1986 to 2000. The rate of growth in the share of women graduates during that time was 4.3 percent, very similar to that of women into the Dental Corps and women

---

[2] L. Jackson Brown, "Dental Work Force Strategies During a Period of Change and Uncertainty," *Journal of Dental Education*, Vol. 65, No. 12, 2001.

[3] Nominal data are from Albert H. Guay, "Dental Practice: Prices, Production, and Profits," *Journal of the American Dental Association*, Vol. 136, No. 3, 2005. Inflation adjustment was made using a CPI calculator (Institute for the Measurement of Worth, Measuring Worth, Web page, 2009).

[4] For example, the median wage of general internists in May 2007 was $167,270 and for prosthodontists it was $169,360 (see U.S. Department of Labor, Bureau of Labor Statistics, Occupational Employment Statistics, "Occupational Employment and Wages, May 2007," Web page, April 2008).

[5] Annual data on gender in the Air Force come from data extracts from the U.S. Air Force Personnel Center, Air Force Personnel Statistics, Web page, 2009. Data on women graduating from dental school come from the DHHS Web page, no date, Table 308: First-Year and Total Enrollments and Graduates in Dental Schools by Gender, Academic Years: 1985–1986 to 2000–2001.

in the Officer Corps. The annual percentage of women entering the Dental Corps, in the Officer Corps (percentage of total population), and graduates of U.S. dental schools is displayed in Figure 4.3.

There have been three distinct phases of entry into the Dental Corps for racial minorities. During the early period, very few racial minorities entered the Dental Corps. The data show that from 1978 to 1990, only 40 Asian Americans and a combined 35 African Americans, Hispanics, and Native Americans entered the Dental Corps. There appears to have been rapid growth of all minorities during the 1990s. During that period, the reported combined share of minorities grew to around 20 percent per year. In the third phase, after 2000, the reported share of all minorities declined sharply to around 13 percent per year. The observed decline may not have represented a true decrease, however, but more likely reflected changes in the classification system (for example, the addition of the "decline to state" and "other" categories). Further, the small combined sample size of these groups makes year-to-year comparisons problematic. Unfortunately, data on the

Figure 4.3
Female Graduates of U.S. Dental Schools, Entry of Women into the Dental Corps, and Women in the Air Force Officer Corps, 1975–2007

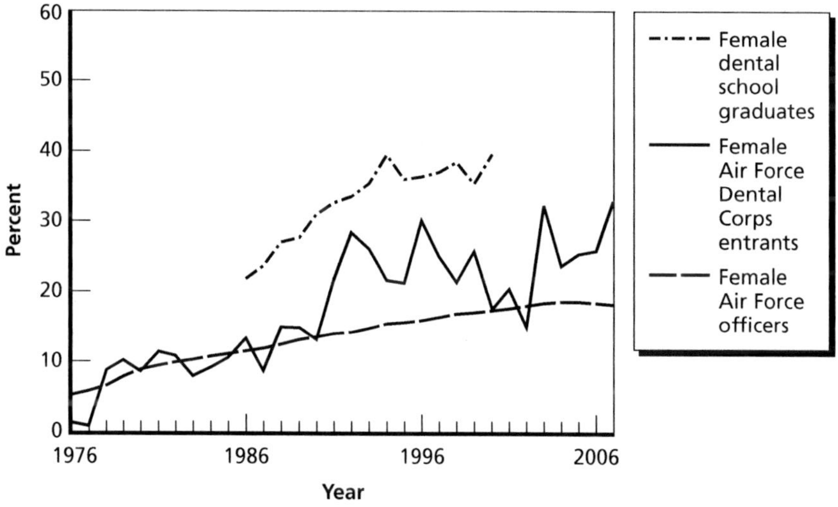

RAND *MG866-4.3*

percentage of minorities graduating from U.S. dental schools were not readily available for comparison.

Dentists were much more likely to enter the Air Force as generalists than were physicians. Between 1978 and 1988, 94 percent of dentists entered as dental officers (982X)[6] or general clinical dentists (982XC), designations that corresponded to entry-level generalists. Specialties that required advanced residency training (including orthodontics, oral surgery, and pediatric dentistry) each made up less than 1.5 percent of all entering cohorts during this period.

While the vast majority of dentists entered as general dentists, a sizable number underwent residency training while in the Dental Corps. Table 4.1 shows the percentage of entering dental officers and general clinical dentists who finished with different specialties.

As Table 4.1 illustrates, more than 28 percent of entering general clinical dentists and more than 40 percent of entering dental officers finished their careers in the Dental Corps with a different specialty (some switching occurred between these two categorizations as well). For entering dental officers, 9.8 percent finished their careers as comprehensive dentists, 3.8 percent finished as periodontists, and 4.3 percent finished as oral surgeons. Between 3 and 4 percent of entering general clinical dentists switched into advanced clinical dentistry (general clinical dentistry plus a two-year residency), comprehensive dentistry, endodontics, oral surgery, or orthodontics.

Dental Corps Retention

The retention of dentists has become a major source of concern in recent years. As we illustrated in Figure 1.4, the annual overall attrition from the Dental Corps trailed Medical Corps attrition through the 1980s and most of the 1990s but has exceeded Medical Corps attrition in more recent years.

---

[6] Note that the AFSCs changed in 1993. After 1993, a dental officer was be classified as a 47GX and a general clinical dentist was classified as a 47GXC.

Table 4.1
1978–2000 Entering Dental Officers and General Clinical Dentists, by Finishing Specialty (%)

	Final Specialty					
Entering Specialty	Advanced Clinical Dentist	Comprehensive Dentistry	Dental Officer	Endodontist	General Clinical Dentist	Oral Surgeon
Dental Officer	3.11	9.75	**59.92**	2.28	9.85	4.27
General Clinical Dentist	3.59	3.23	7.19	3.13	**71.80**	3.50

Table 4.1—continued

	Final Specialty				
Entering Specialty	Orthodontist	Other	Pediatric Dentistry	Peridontist	Prosthodontist
Dental Officer	2.37	1.11	0.74	3.76	2.83
General Clinical Dentist	3.04	0.37	0.74	2.12	1.29

The retention of all HPSP entrants at seven years was, on average, lower than that of direct accessions. For the sample of entrants from 1978 to 2000, 29 percent of HPSP entrants stayed for longer than seven years compared with 43 percent of direct accessions. However, because HPSP entrants are much more heavily concentrated in later cohorts, it is possible that much of the observed change is driven by some exogenous time-related factor rather than by some intrinsic characteristic of HPSP entrants or the HPSP program.

To get a better comparison, Figure 4.4 shows the percentage of entrants in HPSP and direct accessions from 1978 to 2000 who stayed longer than seven years (HPSP entrants were not plotted from 1982 to 1993 because only six HPSP graduates entered in those years, making the sample sizes too small for comparison). For direct accessions, the trend in seven-year retention was variable from year to year but not clearly downward. For HPSP, by contrast, the trend was quite clearly downward, beginning in 1997. This strongly suggests that most of the downward trend in seven-year retention observed in these cohorts is accounted for by HPSP entrants (particularly since they

Figure 4.4
Dental Corps HPSP and Direct-Accession Entrants' Seven-Year Retention Percentages

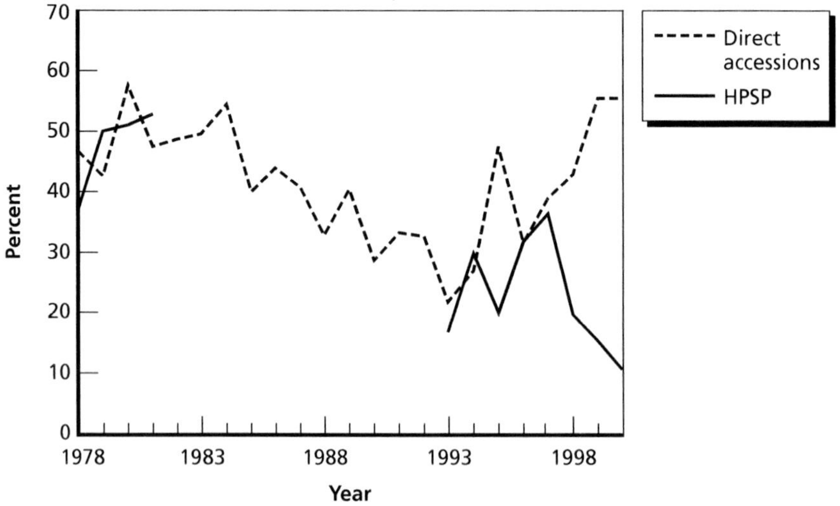

RAND *MG866-4.4*

became the majority of entrants in the mid-1990s). However, we still cannot infer that the HPSP program by itself was the primary cause of decreased retention. The change could have been mediated by some unmeasured time-dependent variable.

To get a sense of the changing points of attrition over time, we calculated the retention of entering cohorts at three years (the point of the highest attrition), seven years, and nineteen years (the months immediately preceding first pension eligibility).[7] We would expect these three points to co-vary: If a dentist had not been retained at three years, that dentist by definition would not be retained at seven or nineteen years either, lowering the average percentage retention for all three. As Figure 4.5 illustrates, although the three measures did increase and decrease

Figure 4.5
Percentage Retention of Dental Corps at Three, Seven, and Nineteen Years, 1978–2004 Entrants

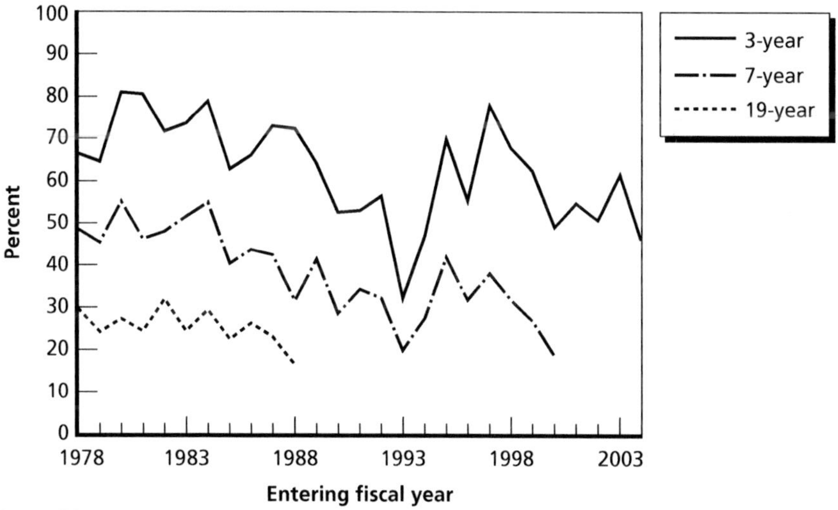

RAND *MG866-4.5*

[7] It is not sensible to plot the percentage of dentists who are still present 20 years after their first year in the Dental Corps. By the 20th anniversary of the first time we see a dentist in the data, a number of dentists will have already retired. Hence, the 19-year retention rate is, in fact, a better measure of the percentage of an entering cohort that will serve 20 years in the Dental Corps.

together, the magnitude of change varied. Three-year retention was a much more volatile measure than seven-year or nineteen-year retention. This suggests that, although short-term attrition changed a great deal over time, the probability of being retained over the longer term changed much less.

The 1993 entering cohort had unusually low three- and seven-year retention rates (32 percent and 20 percent, respectively), although the 2000 entering cohort had yet-lower seven-year retention (18.5 percent).

Figure 4.5 also shows the nineteen-year retention of dentists through 1988 (the last cohort for which we have that many years of observation). The average retention of dentists at nineteen years was much higher than that of physicians. Of all dentists entering from 1978 to 1988, 26.5 percent stayed for longer than nineteen years compared with 12.7 percent of all physicians from the same time period. We also examined whether retention at three, seven, and nineteen years was affected by gender, race, or specialty field. Our findings are presented in Table 4.2. For each retention outcome, we looked at the longest time series possible: For retention at three years, we looked at entering cohorts up to 2004; for seven-year retention, we looked at entering cohorts up to 2000; and for nineteen-year retention, we looked at entering cohorts up to 1988. The denominator of each cell is therefore different. For example, the percentage of men retained at three years is out of the 2,563 men who had entered from 1978 to 2004, whereas the percentage of men retained at seven years is out of the 2,360 men who had entered from 1978 to 2000. Therefore, the second column in a row contains more years of data than the third column, and the third more than the fourth. Further, the columns are not independent. All the dentists in the fourth column of a row are, for instance, in the second and third columns.

Comparing the retention of men and women, we find that men and women had very similar retention at three years. Between Years 3 and 7, however, the retention of men was much higher. By Year 7, the retention of men was more than ten percentage points higher. Partially because of their lower seven-year retention, the retention of women was also lower at Year 19. Table 4.2 does not adjust for time effects, and

Table 4.2
Dental Corps Retention at Three, Seven, and Nineteen Years, by Gender, Race, and Final AFSC

	Percentage Retained at 3 Years, 1978–2004 Cohorts (Number)	Percentage Retained at 7 Years, 1978–2000 Cohorts (Number)	Percentage Retained at 19 Years, 1978–1988 Cohorts (Number)
Gender			
Men	64.87% (1,738)	42.58% (1,005)	27.16% (407)
Women	62.15% (312)	32.43% (131)	20.96% (35)
Race			
Underrepresented minority (Black/Hispanic/Native American)	70.17% (120)	49.09% (27)	26.23% (16)
Asian	67.68% (111)	57.52% (65)	20.00% (6)
White non-Hispanic	64.90% (1,701)	39.88% (1,012)	24.69% (402)
Final AFSC			
Generalist/ no residency	49.57% (1,051)	18.68% (329)	9.27% (99)
Generalist/ residency	97.17% (379)	95.08% (309)	84.19% (181)
Specialist	92.85% (611)	83.75% (469)	41.49% (156)

since women were more heavily concentrated in later cohorts (which had higher attrition across the board), the gender disparity may also reflect these time-related effects.

Underrepresented minority dentists (Blacks, Hispanics, and Native Americans) had higher retention than white non-Hispanic dentists at all three points of time. This is consistent with our earlier finding for the Medical Corps (Tables 2.3 and 2.4), which showed that the retention of underrepresented minority physicians was higher than that of white non-Hispanic physicians. Asian dentists had slightly higher retention rates than white non-Hispanics and slightly lower rates than other minorities at three years. Asians had the highest retention at seven years but trailed the other groups at nineteen years. Although there were differences between minorities and whites, the differences were not substantial. Classification of minority groups was probably imprecise in earlier years, and the sample sizes were relatively small. Either of these factors would reduce the precision of these results.

We also examined the relationship between final AFSC and retention, looking at three different groups: generalists who left the Dental Corps without completing a residency (dental officers and general clinical dentists), generalists who left with a residency completed (comprehensive dentists and advanced clinical dentists), and specialists (e.g., orthodontists, endodontists, oral surgeons). As discussed earlier, a sizeable proportion of dentists entered without a residency completed and trained further in general dentistry or obtained a specialty while serving in the Air Force. However, to leave with a residency-qualified specialty, the dentist needed to have spent time in a residency program, acquiring more service years in the process. Not surprisingly, the retention of those who left without a residency was much lower than that of the residency-qualified generalists and the specialists. The gap widened over time. For example, only 9.3 percent of general dentists who left without completing a residency stayed for longer than nineteen years compared with 84.2 percent of general dentists who left with a residency completed. Although the retention of generalists who left with a residency completed and dentists who left with a specialty was quite similar at three years, generalists with a residency completed had a higher retention at seven years and nineteen years. One possible explanation for this finding is that specialists were more likely to leave for civilian careers because they had higher income opportunities in the private sector than did generalists who completed a residency.

Dental Corps Promotion

As with the Medical Corps, we can only infer officers' promotion points using the personnel data. We cannot determine with certainty when an officer was considered for promotion, limiting our ability to make definitive statements about the timing of promotions.

As is also true of physicians, dentists are exempt from DOPMA constraints on the number of majors, lieutenant colonels, and colonels allowed on active duty in the Air Force. Over 97 percent of all Dental

Corps entrants from 1978 to 2000 entered as captains (O-3). Around 2.6 percent entered as majors (O-4). A very small minority (less than 0.2 percent) entered as lieutenant colonels (O-5) or higher.

Whereas most physicians were promoted from captain to major within three years of completing their residencies, the situation for dentists was quite different. For all Dental Corps entrants, regardless of their accession characteristics, the most common time for promotion to major was six years. Of the 1,667 dentists who entered the Dental Corps between 1978 and 1988, 901 (54 percent) were promoted to major, and the remainder left the Dental Corps as captains. Of the 901 who were promoted from captain to major, 63.6 percent reached this promotion point in their sixth year. Relatively few (less than 3 percent) took longer than six years. The remaining one-third of the dentists promoted were promoted to major in less than six years. The high proportion of early promotions may have been caused by many direct-accession dentists receiving constructive credit for their civilian experience.

Promotion to major was slower for dentists who entered in an Air Force training program (AFSC ending in "1"; only a small share of these trainees would immediately transition into residencies). For entering trainees, fewer than 23 percent reached the grade of major in less than six years. By comparison, for those who did not enter as trainees, 40 percent reached major before their sixth year.

The only two accession categories that could be compared for promotion to major were direct accessions and HPSP. To gain a large enough sample size, we examined promotions from captain to major from 1978 to 1998 (rather than from 1978 to 1988). During this time, 1,058 direct accessions and 132 HPSP entrants gained promotion from captain to major. On average, the HPSP entrants were promoted more slowly than direct accessions. Thirty-five percent of direct accessions were promoted to major in less than six years, compared with 21 percent of HPSP graduates. Direct-accession dentists with constructive credit for civilian experience would be one explanation for this result.

In the sample of entrants from 1978 to 1988, the promotion of women to major was slower than that of men, even after controlling for whether the dentist entered in a training program. Just over 15 percent of female entrants reached major in less than six years, compared with 35 percent of men. This finding should be qualified; the sample size was somewhat limited (only 85 women joined the Dental Corps between 1978 and 1988). This trend did not persist over time: Women entering in the next decade (1989–1998) were promoted from captain to major at roughly the same speed as men.

In the sample of entrants from 1978 to 1988, 605 made it to lieutenant colonel. The majority of majors (66 percent) stayed on and attained the rank of lieutenant colonel. For entrants from 1978 to 1988, conditional on entering as a captain, the most common time to promotion from major to lieutenant colonel was six years (84 percent). Eight percent were promoted in fewer than six years, and the remaining 7.5 percent took more than six years.

Of the 605 Dental Corps officers promoted from major to lieutenant colonel, 43 were women and 562 were men. The time to promotion for men was slightly faster: 13.4 percent made it to lieutenant colonel in less than six years after becoming major, compared with less than 5 percent of the women. However, as with promotion to major, the difference disappeared for entering cohorts between 1989 and 1998. Since only 19 racial minority dentists were promoted to lieutenant colonel from 1978 to 1988, we did not attempt a comparison with white non-Hispanic dentists for this time period. Examining a longer time series, 1978–1998, when there were 55 minority dentists, we find that minorities were promoted slightly more slowly than white non-Hispanics (7.3 percent in less than six years compared with 12.6 percent). Again, these data should be interpreted with caution because of the small sample size.

In the entering cohorts from 1978 to 1988, there were 332 promotions from lieutenant colonel to colonel. As with promotions from major to lieutenant colonel, the most common time to promotion from lieutenant colonel to colonel was six years after becoming a lieutenant colonel (84.0 percent). Of the promotions to colonel, 5.4 percent took place in fewer than six years; the remaining 10.5 percent took longer than six years. A dentist who reached each promotion point (captain to major, major to lieutenant colonel, and lieutenant colonel to colonel) at six years would take a combined 18 years to reach colonel. In fact, 52 percent of promotions to colonel took place in Year 18 of a dentist's Air Force career. Almost 6 percent of the dentists took more than 20 years to reach this promotion from the time they entered the Dental Corps. Given this long time horizon, it is quite possible that some dentists who entered in the final years of the 1978–1988 period will be promoted to colonel in 2008 and afterward (and hence be censored from this analysis).

Limited sample size prevented any subgroup analyses of those promoted to colonel. For example, only 23 Dental Corps women were promoted to colonel between 1978 and 1988. Unlike with previous analyses, extending the time series would risk skewing the results (since slower promotion times would be censored in the analysis). We confronted a similar problem in trying to stratify promotions by race and accession source.

With physicians, we found that lieutenant colonels were much more likely than colonels to retire after reaching pension eligibility at Year 20. For dentists, we also found that there is a major difference in retirement between lieutenant colonels and colonels at Year 20: Lieutenant colonels were more than twice as likely to retire in Year 20. However, this difference becomes less pronounced in each year after Year 20. Figure 4.6 on the next page shows the percentage of lieutenant colonels and colonels with careers longer than 19 years to retire in each year.

In the next chapter, we discuss patterns in dentists' eligibility for, and acceptance of, MSP.

Figure 4.6
Percentage of Dentists Retiring in Each Year of Service, Conditional on Staying for More Than 19 Years, 1978–1988 Entering Cohorts

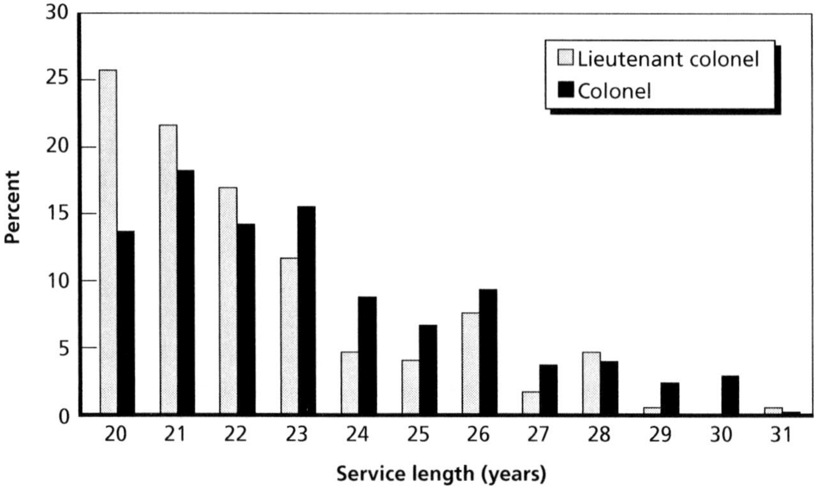

RAND *MG866-4.6*

CHAPTER FIVE

Dentist Cohort Analysis

The responses of dentists to MSP opportunities have been very different from those of physicians. Conditional on becoming eligible for MSP, dentists have accepted DOMRB at much greater rates than physicians. To demonstrate this phenomenon, Figure 5.1 compares the 1995–2000 cohorts of dentists and physicians, aggregating early eligible and later eligible officers in both categories. We ignore the relatively small number of fully qualified direct-accession officers.

Figure 5.1
MSP Acceptance Rates of Eligible Officers, by Entering Cohort

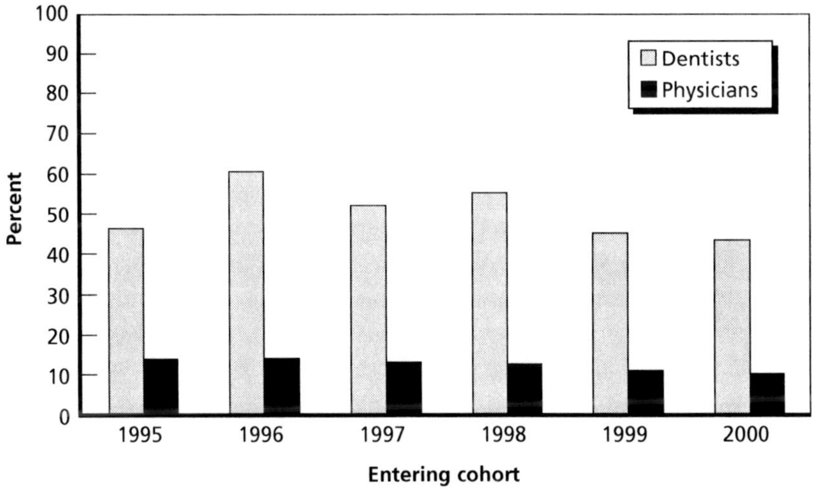

RAND *MG866-5.1*

Roughly half (52 percent) of eligible dentists in these entering cohorts have accepted DOMRB; MSP acceptance rates for physicians were about a quarter of those for dentists.

Most types of dentists first became eligible for DOMRB in FY99, so dentists in the 1995 cohort could not have accepted such MSP until their fourth year of service. For the same reason, Figure 5.1 does not display Dental Corps entering cohorts before 1995; some of those dentists left the Air Force prior to the creation of DOMRB.

We can also analyze eligible dentists' MSP acceptance rate by dental specialty. Figure 5.2 displays these rates for the 1995–2000 cohorts for several larger dental specialties. "Other" aggregates two oral pathologists (Air Force specialty code 47D3), one oral and maxillofacial radiologist (47G3F), twelve periodontists (47H3), and six pediatric dentists (47K3).

Figure 5.2
1995–2000 Entering Cohort DOMRB-Eligible Dentist Acceptance Rates, by Specialty

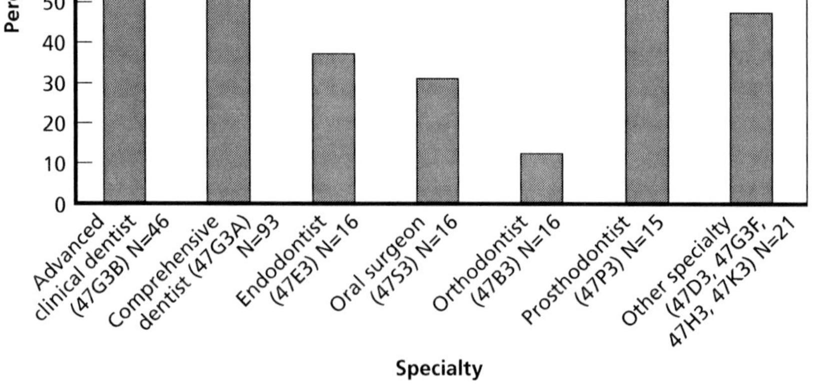

RAND *MG866-5.2*

Advanced Clinical Dentists (47G3B) were most inclined to accept DOMRB; orthodontists (47B3) were least inclined. However, as shown in the specialty labels in Figure 5.2, sample sizes are fairly small—e.g., there were only 15 DOMRB-eligible prosthodontists—so we hesitate to draw much inference from it. Overall, 83 of 139 (59.7 percent) eligible generalists (AFSCs 47G3A and 47G3B) in these cohorts accepted DOMRB, compared with 32 of 84 (38.1 percent) specialists (all other DOMRB-eligible dentists).

While dentists often accept the MSP for which they become eligible, Figure 5.3 shows that most Air Force dentists have not completed residencies that would make them eligible for DOMRB. By contrast, the vast majority of physicians complete such residencies.

Figure 5.4 shows the percentage of each entering cohort's physicians and dentists who had accepted MSP by September 30, 2007. (We removed physicians who were direct accessions and took MSP within their first two years of Air Force service—we are instead interested in

Figure 5.3
1995–2000 Entering Cohort Dentists and Their MSP Status, as of September 30, 2007

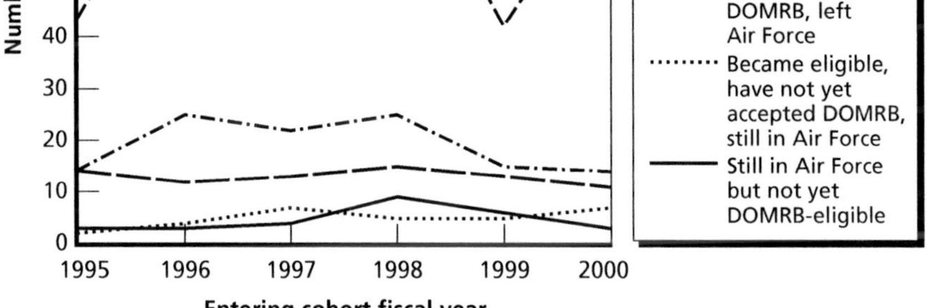

RAND *MG866-5.3*

Figure 5.4
Percentage of Dentists and Physicians Who Have Accepted MSP, by Entering Cohort

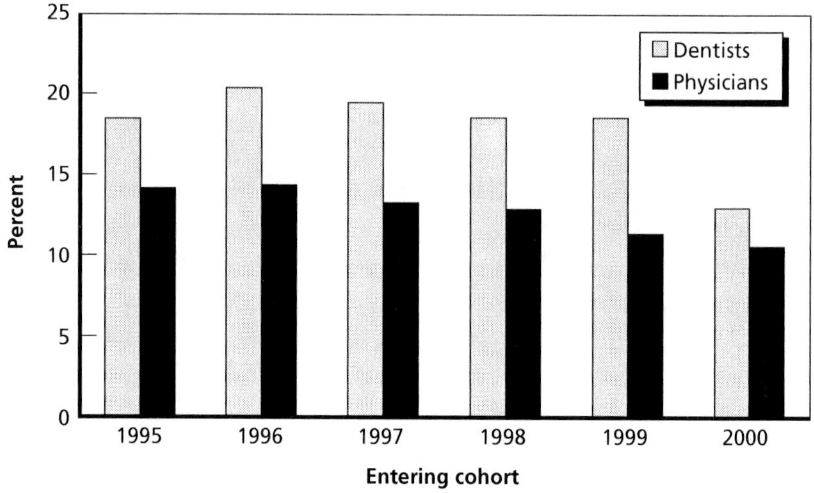

RAND *MG866-5.4*

calibrating the behavior of physicians and dentists who chose between accepting MSP and leaving Air Force service.)

For the 1995–2000 cohorts, a greater percentage of dentists had taken MSP, notwithstanding the fact that many fewer of them completed a residency that would make them eligible for such pay. Also, most dental MSP (DOMRB) was not available until the beginning of FY99.

We want to emphasize the difference between Figure 5.1 and Figure 5.4. Figure 5.1 shows physicians' and dentists' rates of accepting MSP conditional on being eligible for it. Conditional upon eligibility, dentists accept MSP at roughly four times the rate that physicians accept it (52 percent versus 13 percent). Figure 5.4 shows the unfiltered MSP acceptance rate by cohort, including the many dentists who never completed qualifying residencies and who were therefore not eligible- for MSP/DOMRB. Even with that ineligible population included, one still sees that dentists accept MSP at a greater rate than physicians do (18 percent versus 13 percent).

As noted, DOMRB started, for most dental specialties, in 1999. There is no clear evidence from either Figure 1.4 or Figure 4.5 that the existence of DOMRB has reduced overall dentist attrition. Of course, logically, one might believe the adverse trend would have been yet worse absent DOMRB. But a fundamental shortcoming of DOMRB is that it applies to only a minority of dentists. The majority, who do not complete the requisite residency training, are not affected by it (except insofar as the existence of DOMRB encourages them to pursue further training).[1]

Although Figure 1.4 suggests an upward trend in Air Force dentist attrition, Figure 5.5 shows a sharp drop, after the implementation of DOMRB, in the percentage of Air Force dentists within one year of expiration of their service commitment (using the active duty

Figure 5.5
Percentage of Dental Corps Officers Within One Year of Service Commitment Expiration

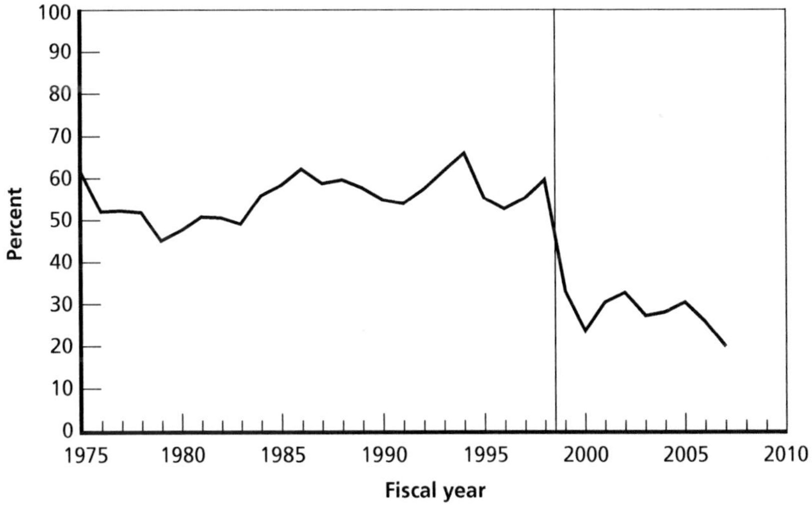

RAND *MG866-5.5*

---

[1] Indeed, one could even hypothesize DOMRB could have an adverse effect on retention of non–residency trained dentists if one believed it has an adverse morale effect due to increased intra–Dental Corps income inequality.

service commitment date [ADSCD] field in the personnel data). For example, September 1995 dentists would have been within one year of service commitment expiration if their ADSCD was September 30, 1996, or earlier. In Figure 5.5, we have superimposed the y-axis at 1999, which is when DOMRB started for most dental specialties.

Prior to DOMRB, more than half of Air Force dentists worked "year to year," impeding planning and increasing ex ante attrition risk. Thus, while actual attrition has not in fact decreased since implementation of DOMRB, there has been a reduced likelihood of short-term, large-scale departure of Air Force dentists.

Next, Chapter Six presents our conclusions, drawing together findings from data on both physicians and dentists.

CHAPTER SIX

Conclusions

At any point in time, there is a stock of physicians and dentists serving in the Air Force. There is also a flow of physicians and dentists in and out of the Air Force—that is, accessions and attrition.

The vast majority of accessions come from a handful of sources:

- New medical and dental school graduates who received HPSP funding for medical or dental school
- New USUHS medical school graduates
- Post-civilian residency physicians who received HPSP support for medical school or FAP support during their residencies.

In the short run, these accession flows are largely predetermined. Even a FAP accession probably made his or her commitment to Air Force service three or more years ago. An HPSP physician who served a civilian residency may have committed to Air Force service ten or more years ago.

The largely predetermined nature of Medical and Dental Corps accessions has important force management implications. In particular, if the Air Force wants to increase the Medical or Dental Corps populations, the only clear-cut short-run tactic would be to reduce the attrition rate of physicians and dentists whose service commitments are about to expire.[1]

[1] The challenge is less constrained if the desire is to reduce the population. Along with letting physicians and dentists with expiring commitments leave, the Air Force could waive or reduce service commitments for existing or incoming physicians and dentists.

MSP, a major focus of this paper, is intended to keep physicians and dentists in the Air Force after their initial service obligations have expired. MSP has been particularly successful in that eligible dentists have often accepted it. Most eligible physicians have heretofore refused MSP, instead choosing to leave the Air Force, but some physicians, most notably those who received their residency training at military medical centers, have shown a growing inclination to accept it. Of course, we cannot observe the counterfactual as to how many physicians or dentists who accepted MSP would have stayed in the Air Force regardless. Nevertheless, as documented in Appendix C, we find evidence that physician MSP "works," at least in the narrow sense that increasing MSP levels appears to increase the percentage of physicians who choose to accept MSP versus leaving Air Force service.

Figure 1.2 suggested Air Force physician accessions have trended downward in recent years while dentist accessions have been static. On the other hand, Figure 1.4 suggested physician attrition has been near historic lows in recent years while dental attrition has been increasing.

One way to think about the futures of the Medical and Dental Corps is to imagine that the Air Force is in a steady state, i.e., each Corps' population was constant over time. In a steady state, the baseline population multiplied by the attrition rate (i.e., the number of departing physicians or dentists) equals the number of accessing physicians or dentists. Or, put differently, each Corps' steady-state population equals its number of annual accessions divided by its attrition rate.

Figure 6.1 shows three lines or isoquants. On the highest line, we have connected the possible combinations of annual accessions and attrition rates consistent with a steady-state Medical Corps population of 3,000 physicians. The line slopes up, i.e., if the Medical Corps has more accessions, it can tolerate greater attrition.

The lower isoquants in Figure 6.1 are for greater Medical Corps steady-state populations of 3,500 and 4,000. To have a greater steady-state population, the Air Force needs either more Medical Corps accessions or a lower average annual attrition rate (or both).

We have also superimposed icons showing the 2007 Medical Corps accession and attrition combination (342 accessions, 10.6 percent attrition) as well as the 2000–2007 average accession and attrition

Figure 6.1
Air Force Medical Corps Steady-State Calculations

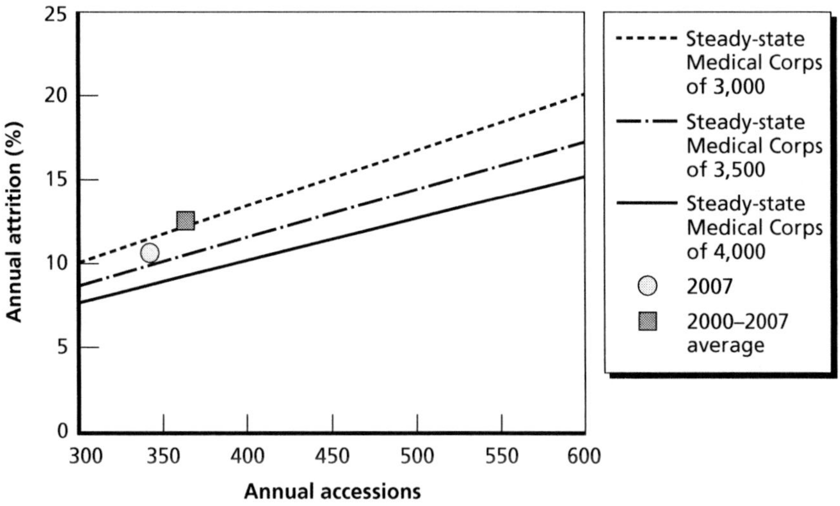

RAND *MG866-6.1*

combination (364 accessions, 12.4 percent attrition). The 2007 combination is consistent with a steady-state Medical Corps size of 3,234 physicians; the 2000–2007 combination is consistent with a steady-state Medical Corps size of 2,926 physicians. But the actual FY07 Medical Corps population was 3,411 physicians. It would appear that, absent some changes in accession or attrition behavior, the Medical Corps shrinkage depicted in Figure 1.1 will continue.

The findings for the Dental Corps, as shown in Figure 6.2, are similar.

The 2007 Dental Corps combination of 97 accessions and 13.6 percent attrition is consistent with a steady-state Dental Corps size of 715 dentists, but the actual 2007 Dental Corps population was 901 dentists. As with the Medical Corps, we project continuing shrinkage in the Dental Corps absent either increased accessions or reduced attrition.

We recommend the Air Force focus on increasing Medical Corps accessions. Still further increases in MSP could further reduce Medical Corps attrition. The large population of HPSP accessions who currently generally do not stay past their initial obligation is a target of

Figure 6.2
Air Force Dental Corps Steady-State Calculations

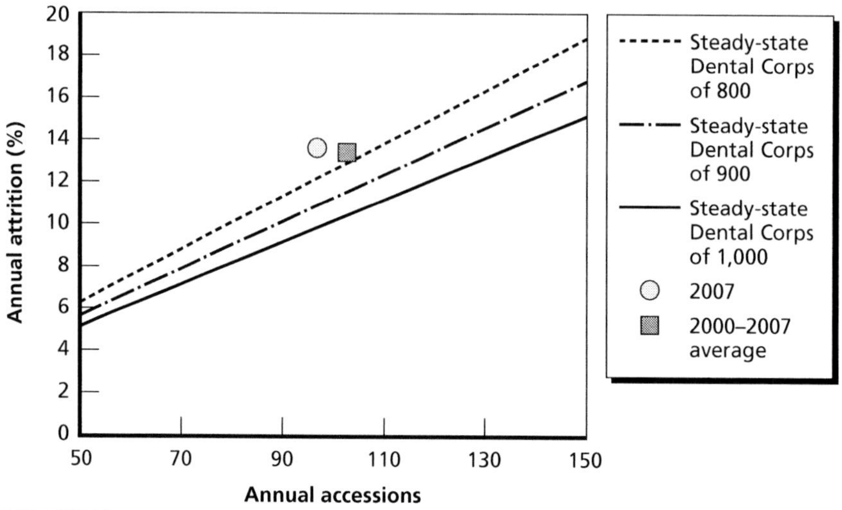

RAND *MG866-6.2*

opportunity. However, a sizable increase in retention of that population would result in an increasingly senior Medical Corps over time. If the Air Force wishes to maintain its current Medical Corps seniority structure, accessions must be increased or at least stabilized.

The Dental Corps situation is quite different. The good news is that accessions have been static and that eligible dentists often accept DOMRB. The challenge with the Dental Corps is that the majority of Air Force dentists do not obtain the residency training required for DOMRB eligibility.

We urge the Air Force to consider retention bonuses for dentists who have not yet completed residencies that make them eligible for DOMRB. Dental Corps accessions have been variable from year to year but have not shown the decrease seen in the Medical Corps. DOMRB-eligible dentists are being retained at a high rate. The hole in the Dental Corps' portfolio lies in retaining dentists who have not completed DOMRB-qualifying residencies.

Table 6.1 summarizes our findings and recommendations.

Table 6.1
Summary of Findings and Recommendations

Category	Physicians	Dentists
Accessions	Trending downward	Static
Attrition	Near historic lows	Variable but trending up
Acceptance of MSP/DOMRB	Increased in recent years	About 50%, conditional on eligibility
Recommendation	Focus on increasing accessions	Increase retention incentives for dentists not eligible for DOMRB

APPENDIX A

Estimating a Physician's or Dentist's Eligibility for Multiyear Special Pay

According to Financial Management Regulation Volume 7A, Chapter 5, a Medical or Dental Corps officer is eligible for MSP if he or she has completed

- appropriate residency training (civilian or military)
- at least eight years of creditable service OR any active duty service obligation incurred for medical education and training.[1]

Unfortunately, there is no indicator in the personnel data that we received to show if and when a physician or dentist became eligible for MSP.[2] We instead had to estimate such eligibility on an officer-by-officer basis.

Of course, the clearest indicator that a physician or dentist is MSP-eligible is seeing in the payroll data that the physician or dentist received MSP. However, we also wanted to estimate the MSP eligibility of physicians and dentists who became eligible for such pay but chose not to accept it.

---

[1] Office of the Under Secretary of Defense (Comptroller), DoD Financial Management Regulation, Volume 7A, Chapter 5, February 2002.

[2] Our April 2008 discussions at the AFPC suggested that it was developing an automated process to determine an officer's MSP eligibility. But AFPC's efforts were forward-looking and could not help us with our challenge to ascertain when, in the past, a physician or dentist who may no longer be in the Air Force became eligible for MSP.

However, payroll data on MSP receipt provided by the Defense Manpower Data Center (DMDC) were quite helpful to us because we could use them to check our algorithm development. We wanted an MSP-eligibility determination algorithm that correctly categorized those physicians and dentists who, in fact, received MSP without grossly exaggerating eligibility.

Five variables in the AFPC-provided personnel data file provided clues as to the eligibility of physicians and dentists who did not accept MSP. Those variables were the officer's accession source, the officer's PAFSC, the officer's duty Air Force specialty code (DAFSC), the graduate professional education (GPE) indicator, and the ADSCD. An officer's PAFSC, DAFSC, GPE, and ADSCD can vary by fiscal year; his or her accession source does not.

For physicians, we found the payroll data on MSP receipt generally supported an algorithm that "appropriate residency training" had been completed once a PAFSC with a "3" in the fourth slot (or "duty level") is observed, e.g., 44F3 (family practice physician), 45S3 (general surgeon), 44K3 (pediatrician). Also, the graduate professional education variable should be "turned off" (0), a switch that generally occurs when the duty level becomes a "3."[3]

The physician exceptions to the "duty level 3 indicates residency completion" algorithm are 44E3 (emergency services physician), 44G3 (general medical officer), and 48G3 (aerospace medicine physician).[4] We categorize these physicians as not having completed MSP-qualifying residencies unless they have a PAFSC suffix consistent with qualifying residency completion, e.g., 44E3A (emergency medicine specialist).

Along with qualifying residency completion, a physician also needs either eight years of creditable service or to have fulfilled his or her active duty service obligation incurred for medical education and training.

For HPSP and FAP physicians, MSP qualification normally occurs after three or four years of service as a "3." We used the ADSCD

---

[3] Under the pre-1994 AFSC system, the fourth character being a "6" appears to have had the same meaning as the fourth character being a "3" under the current system.

[4] AFSC 9396, 9326, and 9356, respectively, under the pre-1994 system.

in the first year as a "3" to estimate when this commitment expiration occurred. For USUHS physicians, MSP eligibility generally occurs at the eight-year point, almost always preceding the physician's fulfillment of the USUHS educational obligation. Consequently, it is routine and expected for USUHS physicians to continue Air Force service while not accepting MSP when first offered it. See the discussion on pp. 41–42.

Fully qualified physicians without an HPSP, FAP, or USUHS obligation often have an accession source such as "Direct Appointment through the Recruiting Service." These physicians can take MSP upon commencement of their Air Force service.

Our algorithm for estimating dentist MSP (DOMRB) eligibility is similar. Any dentist with a duty level of "3" has completed the requisite residency training, except 47G3 (dental officer) and 47G3C (general clinical dentist). For dentists, the DAFSC can also be informative. In particular, it appears from the payroll data that having either a PAFSC or a DAFSC that is consistent with a qualifying residency completion is sufficient for DOMRB receipt.

The HPSP obligations for dentists are normally fulfilled prior to completion of a qualifying residency. The typical path for an Air Force dentist is to serve for three or four years as a 47G3 or a 47G3C then to either leave the Air Force or to enter a dental residency program (e.g., as a 47S1). Upon completion of that residency program (e.g., the dentist becomes a 47S3, oral surgeon), the dentist is eligible for DOMRB.

We believe that our algorithms do a reasonable job of estimating when physicians and dentists become eligible to accept MSP. That said, there are a fair number of both physicians and dentists who the payroll data indicate received MSP but whom our algorithms estimated not to be eligible. Problems include physicians who we believe have yet-unfulfilled HPSP or FAP obligations and officers with AFSCs inconsistent with eligibility (e.g., 44G3, 47G3) who nevertheless receive MSP. Of course, a certain number of "false negatives" are inevitable unless we want to err in the other direction and deem many officers to be MSP-eligible who, in fact, never were.

We do not believe our "algorithm failures" represent physicians or dentists receiving MSP who did not deserve it. Instead, we believe they suggest a lack of updating in the personnel records—for example a dentist was really a 47G3A but the record we received continues to show a PAFSC and DAFSC of 47G3.

We have made our best efforts to estimate MSP eligibility. We have excluded a number of problematic records. We believe our findings to be adequate for policymaking purposes, but we know our records are not sufficiently accurate to be used for determination of specific officers' MSP eligibility. Fortunately, AFPC and installation-level manpower offices have more-detailed, accurate, and up-to-date data to assist specific officers in their career decisionmaking.

APPENDIX B

Air Force Medical and Dental Special Pays, 1992–2009

The authors were unable to locate a consolidated table of Air Force physician and dentist special pay covering more than a few years. Instead, we constructed such a table ourselves, drawing on Air Force documents, multiple years of the *Uniformed Services Almanac*, and the U.S. Department of Health and Human Services Personnel Manual.[1] We present this information in this appendix. It covers 1992–2009 and focuses on the six largest MSP-eligible physician AFSCs and the six largest DOMRB-eligible dentist AFSCs.

Table B.1 presents the annual MSP levels for Emergency Medicine (44E3A), Family Practice (44F3), and Internal Medicine (44M3) in then-year dollars. Table B.2 presents the annual MSP for OB/Gyn (45G3), Pediatrics (44K3), and Surgery (45S3) in then-year dollars.

Note that Air Force pediatricians were not offered four-year special pay in FY08. Individual military services are allowed to offer only the DoD-prescribed MSP level or no MSP at all. The Air Force was not allowed to offer pediatricians a four-year special-pay level in FY08 less than the DoD-prescribed $25,000. The Air Force offered pediatricians $30,000 in annual MSP for a four-year commitment starting in FY09.

---

[1] DHHS, *Personnel Manual*, Chapter CC22: Pay and Allowance Administration, Subchapter CC22.2: Special Pays, PHS-CC 637, November 10, 1998.

Table B.1
Emergency Medicine, Family Practice, and Internal Medicine Annual MSP (Then-Year $)

	Emergency Medicine (44E3A)			Family Practice (44F3)			Internal Medicine (44M3)		
FY	2-Year	3-Year	4-Year	2-Year	3-Year	4-Year	2-Year	3-Year	4-Year
1992	4,000	8,000	14,000	3,000	6,000	10,000	3,000	6,000	10,000
1993	4,000	8,000	14,000	4,000	8,000	14,000	3,000	6,000	10,000
1994	4,000	8,000	14,000	4,000	8,000	14,000	3,000	6,000	10,000
1995	4,000	8,000	14,000	4,000	8,000	14,000	4,000	8,000	14,000
1996	4,000	8,000	14,000	4,000	8,000	14,000	4,000	8,000	14,000
1997	3,000	6,000	10,000	4,000	8,000	14,000	3,000	6,000	10,000
1998	3,000	6,000	10,000	4,000	8,000	14,000	3,000	6,000	10,000
1999	2,000	4,000	8,000	4,000	8,000	14,000	2,000	4,000	8,000
2000	6,000	7,000	8,000	9,000	10,000	14,000	6,000	7,000	8,000
2001	6,000	7,000	8,000	9,000	10,000	14,000	6,000	7,000	8,000
2002	8,000	9,000	10,000	12,000	13,000	14,000	8,000	9,000	10,000
2003	12,000	13,000	14,000	12,000	13,000	14,000	12,000	13,000	14,000
2004	12,000	13,000	15,000	12,000	13,000	15,000	12,000	13,000	15,000
2005	12,000	13,000	25,000	12,000	13,000	17,000	12,000	13,000	25,000
2006	12,000	13,000	25,000	12,000	13,000	25,000	12,000	13,000	25,000
2007	17,000	25,000	33,000	17,000	25,000	33,000	13,000	19,000	25,000
2008	17,000	25,000	33,000	17,000	25,000	33,000	13,000	19,000	25,000
2009	17,000	26,000	40,000	17,000	25,000	38,000	13,000	23,000	35,000

Table B.2
OB/Gyn, Pediatrics, and Surgery Annual MSP (Then-Year $)

	OB/Gyn (45G3)			Pediatrics (44K3)			Surgery (45S3)		
FY	2-Year	3-Year	4-Year	2-Year	3-Year	4-Year	2-Year	3-Year	4-Year
1992	4,000	8,000	14,000	2,000	4,000	8,000	3,000	6,000	10,000
1993	3,000	6,000	10,000	NA	NA	NA	3,000	6,000	10,000
1994	4,000	8,000	14,000	2,000	4,000	8,000	3,000	6,000	10,000
1995	3,000	6,000	10,000	2,000	4,000	8,000	3,000	6,000	10,000
1996	3,000	6,000	10,000	2,000	4,000	8,000	3,000	6,000	10,000
1997	3,000	6,000	10,000	2,000	4,000	8,000	3,000	6,000	10,000
1998	3,000	6,000	10,000	3,000	6,000	10,000	3,000	6,000	10,000
1999	2,000	4,000	8,000	3,000	6,000	10,000	4,000	8,000	14,000
2000	6,000	7,000	8,000	6,000	7,000	8,000	9,000	10,000	14,000
2001	6,000	7,000	8,000	6,000	7,000	8,000	9,000	10,000	14,000
2002	8,000	9,000	10,000	8,000	9,000	10,000	12,000	13,000	14,000
2003	12,000	13,000	14,000	12,000	13,000	14,000	12,000	13,000	14,000
2004	12,000	13,000	15,000	12,000	13,000	15,000	12,000	13,000	15,000
2005	12,000	13,000	25,000	12,000	13,000	15,000	12,000	13,000	33,000
2006	12,000	13,000	33,000	12,000	13,000	15,000	12,000	13,000	33,000
2007	17,000	25,000	33,000	12,000	13,000	15,000	13,000	34,000	45,000
2008	17,000	25,000	33,000	13,000	19,000	NA	25,000	38,000	50,000
2009	17,000	25,000	35,000	13,000	20,000	30,000	25,000	40,000	60,000

NA = not applicable.

Obviously, in recent years, the MSP levels have escalated considerably. This was not the case in the 1990s. In the 1990s, it was not uncommon for a specialty's MSP drop in nominal terms over time. The expectation that MSP levels will only increase is a recent phenomenon.

Physicians receive other special pays. For example, Additional Special Pay has been $15,000, irrespective of Medical Corps specialty, every year between 1990 and 2009.

Table B.3 provides the annual Incentive Special Pay levels for the six largest Medical Corps specialties. In 2004–2008, there was an additional $5,000 Incentive Special Pay increment for surgeons who were on MSP contracts. In FY09, the surgeon Incentive Special Pay

Table B.3
Emergency Medicine, Family Practice, Internal Medicine, OB/Gyn, Pediatrics, and Surgery Annual Incentive Special Pay (Then-Year $)

FY	Emergency Medicine (44EA)	Family Practice (44F)	Internal Medicine (44M)	OB/Gyn (45G)	Pediatrics (44K)	Surgery (45S)
1992	0	0	0	20,000	0	22,000
1993	10,000	3,000	3,000	25,000	5,000	22,000
1994	16,000	3,000	5,000	24,000	4,000	23,000
1995	15,000	3,000	6,000	29,000	5,000	22,000
1996	18,000	6,000	9,000	29,000	8,000	22,000
1997	18,000	8,000	13,000	31,000	9,000	26,000
1998	18,000	11,000	13,000	31,000	10,000	26,000
1999	20,000	12,000	9,000	31,000	10,000	25,000
2000	22,000	13,000	13,000	31,000	11,000	26,000
2001	22,000	13,000	13,000	31,000	11,000	26,000
2002	26,000	13,000	14,000	31,000	12,000	29,000
2003	26,000	13,000	14,000	31,000	12,000	29,000
2004	26,000	13,000	14,000	31,000	12,000	29,000
2005	26,000	13,000	14,000	31,000	12,000	29,000
2006	26,000	13,000	14,000	31,000	12,000	29,000
2007	26,000	13,000	14,000	31,000	12,000	29,000
2008	26,000	13,000	14,000	31,000	13,000	29,000
2009	26,000	20,000	20,000	31,000	20,000	29,000

multiyear increment leapt to $21,000. Emergency medicine physicians on MSP contracts received a $4,000 increment to their Incentive Special Pay in FY09.

Comparing Table B.3 to Tables B.1 and B.2, we see that in the mid-late 1990s, Incentive Special Pay levels were much greater than MSP levels. In recent years prior to FY09, however, the Incentive Special Pay levels were frozen in nominal terms (and therefore declining in real terms) while there was large-scale growth in the Multiyear Special Pay. Several specialties received Incentive Special Pay increases in FY09.

Table B.4 shows physician Variable Special Pay. The Variable Special Pay table has been unchanged over time except there was an augmented Variable Special Pay of $22,000 per year in 1992 and 1993 for physicians with at least 18 and less than 22 years of creditable service.

Board-certified physicians also receive Board-Certified Pay, as presented in Table B.5.

Table B.4
Physician Variable Special Pay (Then-Year $)

Category	Annual Payment
Undergoing internship	1,200
Less than 6 years of creditable service	5,000
At least 6, less than 8 years of creditable service	12,000
At least 8, less than 10 years of creditable service	11,500
At least 10, less than 12 years of creditable service	11,000
At least 12, less than 14 years of creditable service	10,000
At least 14, less than 18 years of creditable service	9,000
At least 18, less than 22 years of creditable service	8,000[a]
22 or more years of creditable service	7,000
Above pay grade O-6	7,000

[a] $22,000 per annum in 1992 and 1993.

Table B.5
Physician Board-Certified Pay (Then-Year $)

Category	Annual Payment
Less than 10 years of creditable service	2,500
At least 10, less than 12 years of creditable service	3,500[a]
At least 12, less than 14 years of creditable service	4,000
At least 14, less than 18 years of creditable service	5,000
18 or more years of creditable service	6,000

[a] $4,000 per annum in 1992 and 1993.

Physicians' Board-Certified Pay levels have been static since 1994, so they have declined considerably in real terms.

Dentists' special pays are similar, with the most prominent difference being that MSP for dentists did not commence until 1998 for oral surgeons and 1999 for other types of MSP/DOMRB-qualified dentists. Table B.6 presents the MSP levels for advanced clinical dentists (47G3B), comprehensive dentists (47G3A), and oral surgeons (47S3). Table B.7 presents the same information for orthodontists (47B3), periodontists (47H3), and prosthodontists (47P3).

While Tables B.1 and B.2 showed some declines in the nominal value of physician MSP, the newer DOMRBs have not decreased in nominal terms.

Although physician Additional Special Pay has been fixed at $15,000 per year for all physicians since 1990, Dental Corps Additional Special Pay was increased in the late 1990s but was fixed between 2000 and 2008, as shown in Table B.8. Unlike physician Additional Special Pay, dentist Additional Special Pay varies with years of seniority. In FY09, Dental Corps Additional Special Pay was increased for dentists with fewer than ten years of creditable service.

Table B.6
Advanced Clinical Dentist, Comprehensive Dentist, and Oral Surgeon Annual MSP (Then-Year $)

	Advanced Clinical Dentist (47G3B)			Comprehensive Dentist (47G3A)			Oral Surgeon (47S3)		
FY	2-Year	3-Year	4-Year	2-Year	3-Year	4-Year	2-Year	3-Year	4-Year
1992	NA	NA	NA	NA	NA	NA	NA	NA	NA
1993	NA	NA	NA	NA	NA	NA	NA	NA	NA
1994	NA	NA	NA	NA	NA	NA	NA	NA	NA
1995	NA	NA	NA	NA	NA	NA	NA	NA	NA
1996	NA	NA	NA	NA	NA	NA	NA	NA	NA
1997	NA	NA	NA	NA	NA	NA	NA	NA	NA
1998	NA	NA	NA	NA	NA	NA	4,000	8,000	14,000
1999	3,000	6,000	12,000	3,000	6,000	12,000	4,000	8,000	14,000
2000	3,000	6,000	12,000	3,000	6,000	12,000	4,000	8,000	14,000
2001	3,000	6,000	12,000	4,000	8,000	14,000	4,000	8,000	14,000
2002	3,000	6,000	12,000	4,000	8,000	14,000	4,000	8,000	14,000
2003	6,000	8,000	12,000	8,000	10,000	14,000	8,000	10,000	14,000
2004	6,000	8,000	12,000	8,000	10,000	14,000	8,000	10,000	20,000
2005	6,000	8,000	15,000	8,000	10,000	22,000	8,000	10,000	30,000
2006	6,000	8,000	15,000	8,000	10,000	40,000	8,000	10,000	50,000
2007	13,000	19,000	25,000	20,000	30,000	40,000	25,000	38,000	50,000
2008	13,000	19,000	25,000	25,000	38,000	50,000	25,000	38,000	50,000
2009	18,000	27,000	35,000	25,000	38,000	50,000	25,000	38,000	50,000

Table B.7
Orthodontist, Periodontist, and Prosthodontist Annual MSP (Then-Year $)

FY	Orthodontist (47B3)			Periodontist (47H3)			Prosthodontist (47P3)		
	2-Year	3-Year	4-Year	2-Year	3-Year	4-Year	2-Year	3-Year	4-Year
1992	NA	NA	NA	NA	NA	NA	NA	NA	NA
1993	NA	NA	NA	NA	NA	NA	NA	NA	NA
1994	NA	NA	NA	NA	NA	NA	NA	NA	NA
1995	NA	NA	NA	NA	NA	NA	NA	NA	NA
1996	NA	NA	NA	NA	NA	NA	NA	NA	NA
1997	NA	NA	NA	NA	NA	NA	NA	NA	NA
1998	NA	NA	NA	NA	NA	NA	NA	NA	NA
1999	4,000	8,000	14,000	4,000	8,000	14,000	3,000	6,000	12,000
2000	4,000	8,000	14,000	4,000	8,000	14,000	3,000	6,000	12,000
2001	4,000	8,000	14,000	4,000	8,000	14,000	4,000	8,000	14,000
2002	4,000	8,000	14,000	4,000	8,000	14,000	4,000	8,000	14,000
2003	8,000	10,000	14,000	8,000	10,000	14,000	8,000	10,000	14,000
2004	8,000	10,000	14,000	8,000	10,000	14,000	8,000	10,000	14,000
2005	8,000	10,000	22,000	8,000	10,000	22,000	8,000	10,000	22,000
2006	8,000	10,000	35,000	8,000	10,000	35,000	8,000	10,000	40,000
2007	18,000	27,000	35,000	18,000	27,000	35,000	20,000	30,000	40,000
2008	20,000	30,000	40,000	20,000	30,000	40,000	20,000	30,000	40,000
2009	25,000	38,000	50,000	25,000	38,000	50,000	25,000	38,000	50,000

Table B.8
Dental Corps Additional Special Pay (Then-Year $)

FY	<3 Years Creditable Service	3–8 Years	8–10 Years	10–14 Years	14–18 Years	More Than 18 Years
1992	0	6,000	6,000	6,000	8,000	10,000
1993	0	6,000	6,000	6,000	8,000	10,000
1994	0	6,000	6,000	6,000	8,000	10,000
1995	0	6,000	6,000	6,000	8,000	10,000
1996	0	6,000	6,000	6,000	8,000	10,000
1997	4,000	6,000	6,000	6,000	8,000	10,000
1998	4,000	6,000	15,000	15,000	15,000	15,000
1999	4,000	6,000	15,000	15,000	15,000	15,000
2000–2008	4,000	6,000	6,000	15,000	15,000	15,000
2009	10,000	12,000	12,000	15,000	15,000	15,000

Within the Dental Corps, only oral surgeons receive Incentive Special Pay, which started in 2007. Oral surgeon Incentive Special Pay was $25,000 in FY07 and $30,000 in FY08 and FY09.

As shown in Table B.9, while Dental Corps Variable Special Pay has varied with seniority and over time, it has been stable in nominal terms since 2000.

Dental Corps Board-Certified Pay was adjusted in 1997 and has remained fixed in nominal terms since then, as shown in Table B.10.

Table B.9
Dental Corps Variable Special Pay (Then-Year $)

FY	Internship or <3 Years	3–6 Years Creditable Service	6–8 Years	8–10 Years	10–12 Years	12–14 Years	14–18 Years	More Than 18 Years	Above O-6
1992	1,200	2,000	4,000	4,000	6,000	6,000	4,000	3,000	1,000
1993	1,200	2,000	4,000	4,000	6,000	6,000	4,000	3,000	1,000
1994	1,200	2,000	4,000	4,000	6,000	6,000	4,000	3,000	1,000
1995	1,200	2,000	4,000	4,000	6,000	6,000	4,000	3,000	1,000
1996	1,200	2,000	4,000	4,000	6,000	6,000	4,000	3,000	1,000
1997	3,000	7,000	7,000	7,000	6,000	6,000	4,000	3,000	1,000
1998	3,000	7,000	8,000	12,000	12,000	10,000	9,000	8,000	7,000
1999	3,000	7,000	8,000	12,000	12,000	10,000	9,000	8,000	7,000
2000–2009	3,000	7,000	7,000	12,000	12,000	10,000	9,000	8,000	7,000

Table B.10
Dental Corps Board-Certified Pay (Then-Year $)

FY	<3 Years Creditable Service	3–10 Years	10–12 Years	12–14 Years	14–18 Years	More Than 18 Years
1992–1996	0	2,000	2,000	3,000	4,000	4,000
1997–2009	2,500	2,500	3,500	4,000	5,000	6,000

We converted the then-year special pays into constant FY07 dollars using the Bureau of Economic Analysis GDP deflator.[2] As shown in Table B.11, we took the average of the first and second (calendar)

Table B.11
Converting Then-Year Dollars to Constant FY07 Dollars

FY	GDP Deflator, 1st Quarter	GDP Deflator, 2nd Quarter	1st and 2nd Quarter Average	FY07 $ Multiplier
1992	85.72	86.19	85.96	1.3860
1993	87.71	88.19	87.95	1.3546
1994	89.58	89.95	89.77	1.3271
1995	91.53	91.86	91.69	1.2992
1996	93.33	93.66	93.49	1.2742
1997	95.05	95.21	95.13	1.2523
1998	96.09	96.25	96.17	1.2388
1999	97.33	97.67	97.50	1.2219
2000	99.32	99.74	99.53	1.1969
2001	101.48	102.25	101.87	1.1695
2002	103.57	103.94	103.75	1.1482
2003	105.72	106.06	105.89	1.1250
2004	108.18	109.18	108.68	1.0962
2005	111.73	112.45	112.09	1.0629
2006	115.36	116.35	115.85	1.0283
2007	118.74	119.52	119.13	1.0000

[2] U.S. Department of Commerce, Bureau of Economic Analysis, National Economic Accounts, May 16, 2008, Table 1.1.9.

quarter price indexes to form a "fiscal year" average, then estimated a multiplier to normalize nominal values into FY07 terms.

We multiplied the nominal values in Tables B.1 and B.2 to arrive at the FY07 dollar values shown below in Table C.1. For example, the nominal surgery four-year special pay level in 1992 from Table B.2 was $10,000. However, using Table B.11's 1992 multiplier of 1.3860, we arrived at Table C.1's 1992 $13,860 surgery four-year special pay level in FY07 dollars. Of course, since FY08 and FY09 special pay levels were not used in our estimations, we did not translate them into FY07 dollars.

APPENDIX C

Logistic Regression Analysis of Physician Multiyear Special Pay Acceptance

Figures 3.5 and 3.6 suggest a recent upturn in physicians' tendency to accept MSP.

One possible explanation for the apparent increase in MSP acceptance rates is the recent increase in MSP levels. Table C.1 shows the annual two-, three-, and four-year special pay levels for family practice physicians (AFSC 44F3) and surgeons (AFSC 45S3) in constant FY07 dollars.[1] Appendix B presents a more complete tabulation of special pays over time. Certainly increases in MSP levels would be one possible explanation for the increase in MSP acceptance rates. To evaluate this hypothesis, we need to evaluate how the probability of accepting MSP varies as a function of the MSP level. Because the probability of accepting MSP almost certainly also varies with different characteristics of the physician, we need to control for those other characteristics. Logistic regression is an appropriate technique for doing so.[2] Logistic regression is analogous to linear regression in the sense of evaluating the effects of some covariates on the level of an output variable while

---

[1] The MSP values in Table C.1 are not "round numbers" because we have used the Bureau of Economic Analysis' Gross Domestic Product deflator to translate all dollar values into constant FY07 terms. See Table B.11. Also note that Table C.1 runs only through 2007 because the latest military personnel inventory file we analyzed was as of September 30, 2007.

[2] Appendix D discusses the Dynamic Retention Model (DRM). The DRM is a more elegant and theoretically complete way to model military officers' decisionmaking. However, it turns out the DRM is difficult to estimate with the data we have.

Table C.1
Family Practice and Surgery Annual MSP Levels (FY07 $)

	Family Practice (44F3)			Surgery (45S3)		
FY	2-Year	3-Year	4-Year	2-Year	3-Year	4-Year
1992	4,158	8,316	13,860	4,158	8,316	13,860
1993	5,418	10,837	18,964	4,064	8,127	13,546
1994	5,309	10,617	18,580	3,981	7,963	13,271
1995	5,197	10,394	18,189	3,898	7,795	12,992
1996	5,097	10,194	17,839	3,823	7,645	12,742
1997	5,009	10,018	17,532	3,757	7,514	12,523
1998	4,955	9,910	17,343	3,716	7,433	12,388
1999	4,887	9,775	17,106	4,887	9,775	17,106
2000	10,772	11,969	16,757	10,772	11,969	16,757
2001	10,526	11,695	16,373	10,526	11,695	16,373
2002	13,779	14,927	16,075	13,779	14,927	16,075
2003	13,500	14,625	15,750	13,500	14,625	15,750
2004	13,154	14,251	16,443	13,154	14,251	16,443
2005	12,754	13,817	18,069	12,754	13,817	35,074
2006	12,340	13,368	25,708	12,340	13,368	33,934
2007	17,000	25,000	33,000	13,000	34,000	45,000

controlling for other covariates, but it is tailored for the specific framework of a probability that, by definition, falls between zero and one.

Our modeling focuses on a physician's first decision to accept MSP rather than leave the Air Force. That is, we do not analyze the propensity of physicians who have already taken MSP to sign up for additional MSP.[3]

We studied physicians in the 1989–2004 entering cohorts who became eligible to accept Multiyear Special Pay. (There is no value, for instance, in looking at 2004 entering cohort physicians who have not

[3] This limitation in our scope of analysis allows us to treat each decision as statistically independent because each physician is only used once in our modeling. Other, more complex techniques would allow us to use multiple decisions by physicians to evaluate the effect of MSP; however, because the acceptance rate is so small, more-advanced techniques would probably not give us much more information.

yet become eligible for Multiyear Special Pay.) However, the estimation does not consider physicians who are MSP-eligible but who have neither taken MSP nor departed the Air Force as of September 30, 2007. Some physicians do not accept MSP when it is first offered to them, but eventually do so. This phenomenon especially applies to USUHS graduates who face the prospect of end-of-career years without MSP if they choose to accept it immediately upon becoming eligible for it.

The central explanatory variable in our estimation is the four-year special pay amount the physician either took or turned down and left the Air Force. We use the four-year special pay amount as the independent variable. As shown in Table C.1, two- and three-year special pay levels are less than, but positively correlated with, the four-year level. In fact, DMDC pay file data suggest that about 59 percent of the physicians we studied who accepted MSP took the four-year payment and 31 percent took the two-year payment. For the sake of parsimony, we use only the four-year special pay level as an independent variable in our logistic regression. Some of the physicians we identify as MSP takers actually took two- or three-year special pay.

Other independent variables that we explored include the physician's gender, race, accession source, whether he or she is an early or later eligible physician, and his or her specialty.

Table C.2 presents our logistic regression results. In this display, an odds-ratio value greater than 1 suggests increased likelihood of accepting MSP; an odds-ratio value less than 1 suggests decreased likelihood of accepting MSP. The p-values indicate the statistical significance of the variable in the logistic regression and the confidence interval gives an indication of the range of the effect of this variable.

The effect of being female on accepting MSP is not significant, but having this covariate in the model improved the overall fit. We found that nonwhites are significantly more likely to take MSP. HPSP physicians are significantly less likely to take MSP, as are physicians who did civilian, rather than military, residencies, i.e., early eligible physicians are significantly less likely to accept MSP.

Table C.2
Logistic Regression Results

Observations	3489
LR chi2(17)	599.00
Prob>Chi2	0.0000
Pseudo R-Squared	0.1900
Log Likelihood	–1276.5267
Dependent Variable	1: Took MSP 0: Left without taking MSP

Independent Variable	Odds Ratio	P>|z|	95% Confidence Interval	
Four-year special pay level (000s of FY07$)	1.037	0.000	1.02	1.05
Female	0.795	0.067	0.62	1.02
Nonwhite[a]	1.784	0.001	1.31	2.43
Later eligible[b]	4.189	0.000	3.30	5.31
FAP[c]	2.043	0.000	1.39	3.00
Other accession source	3.597	0.000	2.82	4.58
Emergency services (44E)[d]	0.087	0.000	0.05	0.17
ENT (45N)	0.063	0.000	0.02	0.17
Family practice (44F)	0.203	0.000	0.13	0.32
Internal medicine (44M)	0.081	0.000	0.05	0.13
Neurology (44N)	0.022	0.000	0.00	0.17
OB/Gyn (45G)	0.050	0.000	0.03	0.10
Other	0.081	0.000	0.05	0.14
Pathology (44D)	0.221	0.000	0.11	0.46
Pediatrics (44K)	0.156	0.000	0.09	0.26
Psychiatry (44P)	0.127	0.000	0.07	0.24
Radiology (44R)	0.069	0.000	0.04	0.13
Surgery (45S)	0.057	0.000	0.03	0.10

[a] Omitted race is white or Caucasian.

[b] Omitted eligibility status is Early eligible, i.e., completed residency training at a civilian medical center.

[c] Omitted accession status is HPSP.

[d] Omitted specialty is flight surgeons, AFSC 48*3.

MSP acceptance rates vary across specialties; flight surgeons (AFSC 48*3, except for the non–MSP eligible 48G3) are the most favorably inclined. Specialty dummy variable coefficients may reflect the specialties' differential levels of outside opportunity. (In this specification, we assume that those differentials are constant over time.) There are some specialties, however, with too few observations in our data for significant estimation. (Such small specialties are aggregated into "Other" in Table C.2.)

The parameter of most central interest in Table C.2 is the four-year special pay level, a coefficient that is significantly greater than 1, i.e., greater MSP tends to increase MSP acceptance rates.

Our next task was to translate the logistic regression results into estimates of how MSP acceptance rates would vary with different MSP levels.

Each of the 3,489 physicians used in the Table C.2 estimation has specific characteristics, e.g., gender, race, accession source, civilian or military residency, medical specialty. We therefore estimated, for each physician, the probability he or she would have accepted, for instance, $15,000 per year in four-year special pay. We then averaged those physician-specific probability estimates to compute a population-wide estimated average MSP acceptance rate associated with that level of bonus. This approach is what Graubard and Korn term "recycled predictions."[4]

Figure C.1 shows our estimated general relationship (the solid curve) between annual four-year special pay levels (the x-axis) and the probability of accepting MSP (the y-axis). The broken curves show a 95-percent confidence interval around the mean estimate.[5] Not sur-

---

[4] Barry L. Graubard and Edward L. Korn, "Predictive Margins with Survey Data," *Biometrics*, Vol. 55, June 1999, pp. 652–659.

[5] The 95-percent confidence limit for the recycled predictions estimate of the acceptance rate at different MSP amounts was computed using a technique presented in Bradley Efron and Robert J. Tibshirani, *An Introduction to the Bootstrap*, London: Chapman and Hall, 1993. In this methodology, the original data set is resampled and the recycled predictions are made and averaged. This resampling is carried out repeatedly (200 times in our case) and the set of re-sampled estimated predictions is used to estimate the 95-percent confidence interval

Figure C.1
Predicted MSP Acceptance for All MSP-Eligible Physicians, 1989–2004 Cohorts

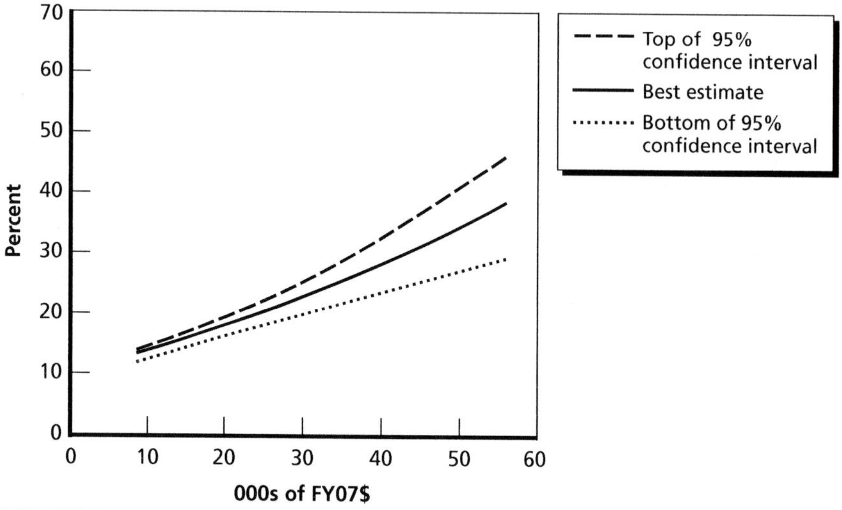

RAND *MG866-C.1*

prisingly, relatively few physicians will accept MSP (and incur the associated additional service commitment) of $10,000 per year, but MSP of $50,000 per year is more attractive.

Figure C.1's best estimate is much less precise at higher MSP levels. As shown in Figure C.2, we have relatively few observations with higher prospective MSP levels. (As noted, we could use MSP levels only through FY07. Since our last personnel inventory was as of September 30, 2007, we do not observe responses to the increased FY08 and FY09 MSP levels.) On the other hand, more than a fifth of total observations in our data set involve four-year special pays between $15,501 and $16,500 (in FY07 terms).

around the original recycled prediction. We applied this technique for a range of prospective MSP amounts; the broken curves were drawn through the derived confidence interval endpoints.

Figure C.2
Percentage of Four-Year Special Pay Observations

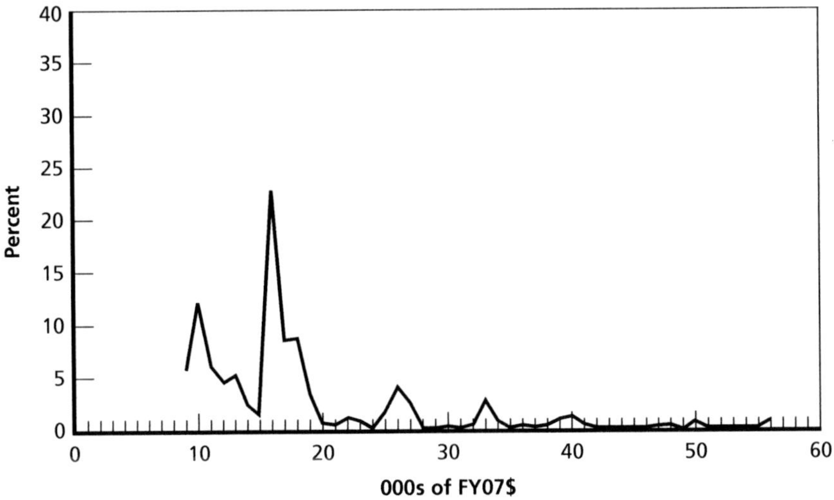

RAND *MG866-C.2*

As shown in the different specialty dummy variable estimates of Table C.2, the attractiveness of MSP varies across specialties. We can use the coefficients in Table C.2 to generate specialty-specific versions of the display in Figure C.1. Figure C.3 shows that family practice physicians (44Fs) are much more inclined to accept MSP of a given level than are surgeons (45S). As in Figure C.1, we have included broken curves showing 95-percent confidence intervals around each specialty's best estimate. The result is not surprising given the greater private-sector income opportunities available to surgeons.

The advantage of recycled predictions is that physicians in each subgroup have the other characteristics representative of that subgroup. For example, if the surgeon group primarily consists of physicians who did military residencies, the method automatically takes that tendency into account.

Figure C.3
Predicted Four-Year MSP Acceptance for Surgeons and Family Practice Physicians, 1989–2004 Cohorts

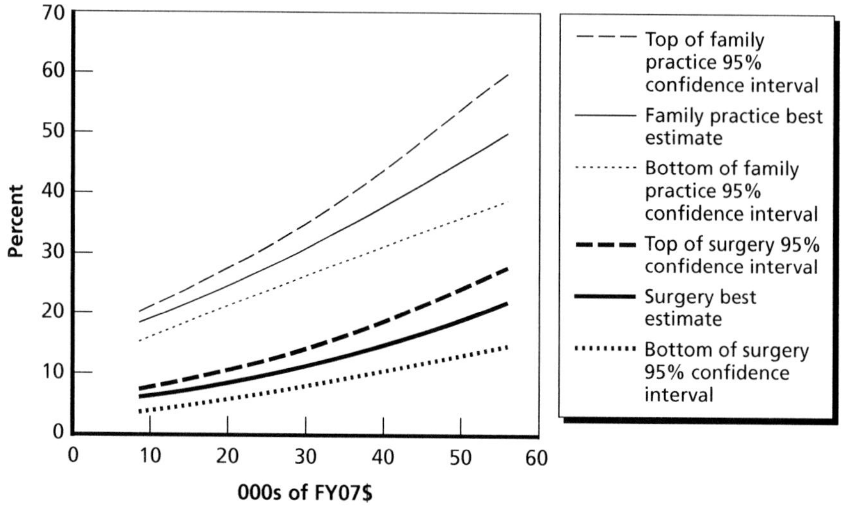

RAND *MG866-C.3*

We urge caution in interpreting these results. For example, as shown in Figure C.4, over the period of our data (1992–2007), family practice physicians were not offered an annual four-year special pay greater than $33,000. Hence, while our technique uses other physicians' responses to estimate how family practice physicians would respond to yet-greater MSPs, such estimates are inherently uncertain.

Also, while the logistic regression in Table C.2 analyzed 3,489 physicians, only 584 accepted MSP. This low overall acceptance rate limited the number of covariates we could use.

Some prospective independent variables were too highly correlated to disentangle. For instance, time and the level of MSP were highly correlated, so we could not compute independent "year effects." It could be that, for instance, other characteristics of the Air Force or the overall economy made multiyear service commitment more attractive in 2006 and 2007 and we are misattributing the increase in acceptance of MSP to increased MSP levels.

Figure C.4
Percentage of Four-Year Special Pay Observations for Family Practice Physicians and Surgeons

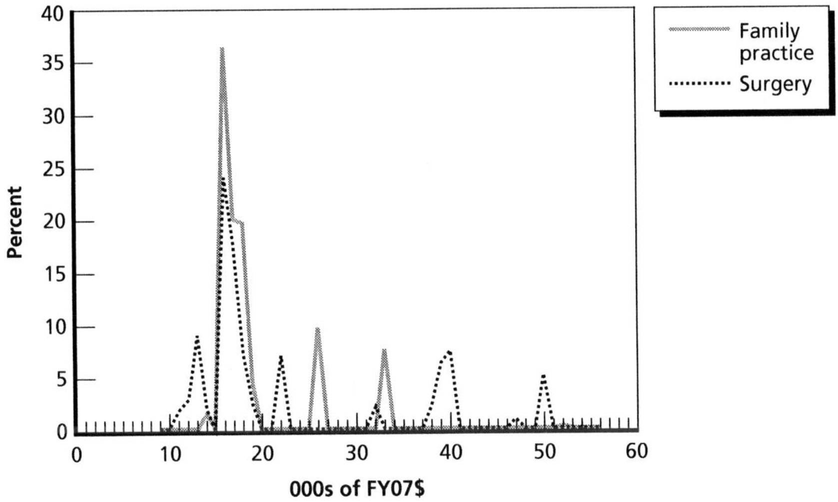

RAND *MG866-C.4*

We note, also, that taking MSP does not necessarily imply a change in attrition behavior. A physician can choose to stay in the Air Force without ever making a multiyear service commitment.

Robustness Checks

We undertook a number of variations of our modeling to assess the robustness of our findings. For example, we ran specialty-specific versions of the logistic regression in Table C.2 (removing, therefore, the specialty dummy variables). The four-year special pay coefficients ranged from 1.03 to 1.15 across the different specialties' logistic regressions. These coefficient estimates were statistically significantly greater than 1 except for Flight Surgeons and Other. The coefficients of the other independent variables (e.g., gender, race, accession source, type of residency) showed considerable differences across the specialty-specific estimations primarily because the mix of women, accession sources, and types of residency is different for different specialties.

We also tried a Table C.2–like logistic regression in which the four-year special pay variable was interacted with specialty dummy variables, thereby estimating multiple specialty-specific four-year special pay coefficients. In this specification, the baseline four-year special pay variable for flight surgeons was not significantly different from 1, nor were most other specialties' four-year special pay variable estimates found to be statistically significantly different from the flight surgeons' baseline. While this result suggests that the physicians in the different specialties do not differ significantly in the effect of the bonus level on their probability of signing up for a bonus, we caution that there is a high correlation between specialty and bonus level (e.g., surgeons generally get higher MSP than family practice physicians), so inclusion of specialty-bonus interaction terms does not work well.

The bottom line is that we have not found significant evidence of differences across specialties in physicians' response to bonuses (i.e., their four-year special pay coefficient) beyond the baseline intercept level of bonus acceptance propensity described in their dummy variable coefficients in Table C.2. It is possible, however, that different specialties, in fact, have different elasticity of response to increased bonus levels, but that our current sample is too small and therefore lacks the power to find these elasticity differences.

We also experimented with a multinomial logit estimation in which we differentiated physicians who took two-year (31 percent of those who accepted MSP), three-year (10 percent of those who accepted MSP), and four-year (59 percent of those who accepted MSP) special pay. All the bonus levels, as in Table C.2, were found to have positive coefficients. The two-year bonus level provided the most attractive bonus amount, i.e., an equal-magnitude increase in all three bonuses would have greatest impact on the number of physicians accepting the two-year bonus. As reflected in the raw number of physicians accepting the bonuses, the three-year choice was estimated to be least attractive.

In the multinomial logit, the other independent variables had similar signs as in Table C.2, e.g., nonwhites are more likely to accept bonuses than whites, HPSP accessions are less likely to accept bonuses than other types of accessions.

Our conclusion is that the multinomial logit requires extra effort and is hamstrung by smaller sample sizes without providing meaningfully different insights than the more straightforward Table C.2 logistic regression.

APPENDIX D

Using the Dynamic Retention Model

One of the tools we considered using in this project was the Dynamic Retention Model (DRM), a sophisticated econometric model that can be used to estimate the retention effects of various pay incentives, including base pay, special pays (including MSP requiring added service commitments), and retirement plans. While this model was formulated in the mid-1980s, its very large computational requirements kept it from being easily used until fairly recently. We were therefore concerned that we might not be able to estimate the model completely and provide comprehensive results; this concern was borne out. However, we did learn about the process of fitting the model and we did get some interesting preliminary results, which we describe in this appendix. We believe that there are a number of directions that can be pursued from this point to facilitate use and expand understanding of the DRM, both in the medical field and for other military career fields.

Introduction

The logistic regression analysis described in Appendix C is a reduced-form model, one that models decisions (either accept MSP or leave) as a nonlinear function of a set of physician characteristics. Additional variables could be utilized, e.g., economic conditions in the year a decision was made (although these may not be as important for physicians' decisions as for the enlisted force), or the effects of important international events, such as the war in Iraq. The result of such a logistic regression is a summary of the empirically observed relationship between MSP acceptance or leaving and other covariates, such as physician characteristics.

The DRM is a more comprehensive and elegant approach to modeling the basic decision process of an individual physician as he or she reaches a decision point, such as the end of a service commitment. The basic theory is that an individual makes a decision to stay or leave the military by comparing the stream of pay available from continuing military service until retirement with that available from moving to the civilian sector, factoring in uncertainty in assignments and other life events, and accounting for personal taste (or lack of it) for military service. The individual then makes the choice that brings the highest reward. This is an economic model of behavior, but it is a model that considers such intangible factors as taste for military service by quantifying or "dollarizing" such factors. Such a behavioral model is valuable for the investigation of personnel responses to changes in pay, bonuses, and retirement plans; its advantage over empirical models such as the logistic regression model is that the compensation schemes studied can be new ones that have never been implemented. In those cases there is no empirical evidence that can be used to construct an empirical model without strong supporting assumptions.

In mathematical terms, at a given time t, the physician can expect to receive the following income if he or she decides to leave the military to enter civilian life:

$$V_t^c = W_t^c + \sum_{\tau=t+1}^{T} \beta^{\tau-t} W_\tau^c + R_t^m + \varepsilon_t^c .$$

V_t^c is the value to the physician of leaving the military and moving into civilian life in year t. W_t^c is the civilian pay the physician would receive over the next year, the summation is the discounted[1] civilian pay stream the physician would receive until retirement in year T, and R_t^m is the military retirement the physician is eligible for if he

[1] The income stream is discounted by a factor $\beta < 1$ because future income is not worth as much as current income. For each future year, the income has to be more discounted because the individual is further from receiving it.

or she leaves at t (0 if t is less than 20 years of service). ε_t^c is a random "shock," the monetary value of a random (positive or negative value) life event in civilian life in the next year.

If the physician chooses to stay in the military for one more year, the value to him or her has the more complex form

$$V_t^m = \gamma_m + W_t^m + \beta E\left\{Max(V_{t+1}^m, V_{t+1}^c)\right\} + \varepsilon_t^m .$$

The civilian pay is replaced by military pay, there is another set of shocks, this time due to positive or negative events in military service, and there is an additional term γ_m, which is the physician's personal taste (in dollars) for military service. Finally, there is the expected value of making a choice in year t + 1, which is the maximum of leaving the military or staying at t + 1, since the physician will have to make the choice to stay or leave again in one year. However, the physician does not know the actual value of the t + 1 choice at time t because there will be future shocks in either civilian or military life that will be positive or negative, so the most that can be done at time t is to look at the expected value of the future choice.

When the choice is across one of several commitment durations, as with MSP, the equation is yet more complex.[2]

As noted above, the physician looks at both of the values and makes the decision that brings the greatest reward: staying in the military if $V_t^m > V_t^c$ and leaving if $V_t^c > V_t^m$. The role of taste is clear: If a person is very committed to military service (has a large, positive taste value), it will take a large amount of civilian pay to induce him or her to leave. Conversely, someone who does not like the military would require substantial amounts of military pay or bonuses to induce him or her to stay.[3]

---

2 For details, see Michael Mattock and Jeremy Arkes, *The Dynamic Retention Model for Air Force Officers: New Estimates and Policy Simulations of the Aviator Continuation Pay Program*, Santa Monica, Calif.: RAND Corporation, TR-470-AF, 2007.

3 The actual mathematics of the decision is somewhat more complex because the physicians must take into account that shocks will occur each year and that accepting a MSP commitment in the military will limit their flexibility and make them vulnerable to several years of

In each of these equations there are several unknowns. We do not know how the physicians perceive the random shocks that they anticipate: Do they expect them to vary widely in size or not? We also do not know the taste for military service of each individual physician. That taste certainly varies by individual characteristics, only some of which we can observe. Moreover, the physician presumably looks ahead over various potential career paths to final retirement, and also has to take into account that accepting longer-term MSP, while more lucrative than a shorter-term commitment, also reduces his or her flexibility.

While we do not know the parameters of the DRM for physicians, we do have the set of data described in this monograph, which shows us the decisions all Air Force physicians made at different stages of their careers. We know when they decided to stay or leave, what MSP they accepted or rejected, and what commitments they made; and we have estimates of what civilian pay was available to them. With these data, we can estimate the values of the unknown parameters that are most consistent with the data we have.

The first forms of the DRM were proposed in the late 1970s.[4] A form specifically for studying the effect of economic factors on military retention was proposed by Gotz and McCall in 1984.[5] However, the limited computing power then available made the estimation of the model very difficult and costly. Therefore, more easily computable approximations to this type of model were found, such as the Annualized Cost of Leaving (ACOL) model.[6] These models, while much more tractable, had known deficiencies in their estimates of person-

---

shocks during which they cannot decide to leave. Details are available in Mattock and Arkes, 2007.

4 Glenn A. Gotz and John J. McCall, *A Sequential Analysis of the Air Force Officer's Retirement Decision*, Santa Monica, Calif.: RAND Corporation, N-1013-1-AF, October 1979.

5 Glenn A. Gotz and John J. McCall, *A Dynamic Retention Model for Air Force Officers*, Santa Monica, Calif.: RAND Corporation, R-3028-AF, December 1984.

6 For example, John T. Warner, *Military Compensation and Retention: An Analysis of Alternative Models and a Simulation of a New Retention Model*, Washington, D.C.: The Center for Naval Analyses, 1981.

nel responses to various economic incentives. The DRM remained the most theoretically appropriate model.

In the late 1990s and early 2000s, computational power had improved so much (and its marginal cost after purchasing the hardware was virtually zero) that estimation of the DRM was much more feasible. A small number of studies have since been done with adaptations of the model.[7]

Although the computations for the DRM are now feasible, for technical reasons (now becoming better appreciated and understood) the estimations are still quite challenging. Also, because of the complexity of the model, the estimates are not available as a single computation. Instead, starting from an initial set of parameter values, those values are changed systematically to bring the model closer and closer to the observed data. There are several potential problems: If the model or the data are complex enough, the estimation process may not be able to get to the best fit to the data from a particular starting point. Instead, the estimation may end up at another place (see below for some examples) because the path to the best fit is not easy to find. Another problem is that the data may not allow us to estimate the values of the unknown parameters accurately enough to be useful, because there are not enough decisions to stay or leave or, as with the physicians, a majority makes the decision to leave at the first decision point. These possibilities complicate the search for the best fit and require multiple runs of the model from different starting points.

Physician Data

To estimate the DRM we need two sets of data. The first is career path data for the personnel used for the estimation. The most important part of these data is the decision made at each decision point and, for those decisions requiring a multiyear commitment, which commitment was made by each physician who stayed. As described in the main body of this monograph, we have yearly snapshots of the Medical Corps that

[7] For example, Mattock and Arkes, 2007.

include demographic data. However, we found the fields that purportedly indicate what commitment was made to be too unreliable for our use.[8] We therefore merged our personnel data with DMDC pay data allowing us to infer which commitment a physician made at each decision point.

The second set of data is income data. Basic military pay by grade is available from the *Uniformed Services Almanac*. Physician special pays were collected from various AF/SG and AF/A1 sources (current pays are, of course, easy to acquire, but we required the complex special pays back to 1995, presented in Appendix B). Civilian compensation figures were hardest to acquire, because there are competing surveys and research organizations producing variants of these amounts. We used the *2007 Review of Physician Recruiting Incentives*.[9] All dollar amounts were converted to 2007 dollars.

Modifying and Running the DRM

The Mattock-Arkes Implementation

As noted above, Mattock and Arkes (2007) produced an implementation of the DRM to model pilot retention, and used the model in several studies for the Air Staff on the retention effect of aviation bonuses. Unlike the earlier Gotz-McCall implementation, which was written in FORTRAN, they elected to use the statistical programming language R.[10] R is an interpreted language, which means it is less computationally efficient than a compiled language, such as FORTRAN or C++, but the order-of-magnitude increases in computing power since the mid-1980s, plus zero-marginal cost computing, meant that the R implementation was at least as efficient as the older FORTRAN ver-

---

[8] See Mattock and Arkes, 2007, for similar problems with aviation personnel data.

[9] Merritt Hawkins and Associates, *2007 Review of Physician and CRNA Recruiting Incentives*, Irving, Tex.: Merritt Hawkins and Associates, 2007.

[10] R is an open-source version of the statistical programming language S, which was developed by AT&T Bell Labs in the 1980s. See R Development Core Team, The R Project for Statistical Computing, Web site, no date.

sion. Further, using R allowed access to superior facilities for debugging and program development, as well as to standard functions for integration and optimization. Results from the simulation could also be plotted and analyzed in R.

The data set of pilots used by Mattock and Arkes was somewhat different from the physician data set we used. First, bonus amounts and policies had changed little over the years of pilot data available to Mattock and Arkes. Therefore, the only time element of interest in their problem was the years of service for each person, not the actual calendar year in which a person made a stay-or-leave decision. However, they could determine from their data only whether a pilot was in the force or not, not whether he or she had taken any one of several bonus options. For each career path, their model therefore had to generate series of paths (essentially bonus choices) that were consistent with their presence in the force. These characteristics resulted in a program that was somewhat specialized to the pilot data set.

The actual optimization was controlled by the R function *optim,* which takes a user-defined function (in this case, the probabilities of making the observed decision for each person in the data set as a function of the unknown parameters) and finds the parameter values that produce the maximum value (in this case finding the parameters which make the model most consistent with the observed data), using one of a set of algorithms selected by the user. Mattock and Arkes used two successive algorithms. First, they used simulated annealing, which begins by generating large stochastic changes in the parameter values and gradually shrinks the size of the changes. This prevents the optimization from ending up in a local maximum and is often useful when the surface to be optimized has an unknown structure, as here.

After a fixed number of simulated annealing steps, the optimization was switched to the Broyden-Fletcher-Goldfarb-Shanno (BFGS) algorithm, which uses both function values and a numerically computed derivative to direct the parameter changes. This process is computationally more intensive than simulated annealing, but it is more efficient at finding the maximum.[11] The program contained provisions for doing several more alternating cycles of simulating annealing and BFGS if the first cycle did not produce a maximum.

Modifying the DRM Model

We elected to continue using R to do our DRM calculations. Starting with the code written by Mattock and Arkes, we modified it substantially in several places to produce a program that was more general and hence better suited to the physician data.[12] These modifications included provision for the special pays to depend on the calendar year of the decision, a general structure for arbitrary covariates for the parameters of the taste distribution, and a more general set of routines for determining the probability of a specific set of decisions. We continued to use the *optim* function with the same alternation of simulated annealing and BFGS.

In addition to the reprogramming, we also constructed test data sets for each set of functions and a spreadsheet to reproduce key DRM calculations so that we could verify that the functions were working correctly.

Estimation Results

We decided to do our initial estimation runs using our data for family practice physicians only; family practice is one of the largest medical specialties in the Air Force. We also decided to estimate only three parameters: the variance of the shock distribution (which describes how much the shocks are expected to range) and the location and spread of the taste distribution for these physicians. Our approach was in contrast to Mattock and Arkes' pilot study, which also included regression

---

[11] See Mordecai Avriel, *Nonlinear Programming: Analysis and Methods*, Mineola, N.Y.: Dover Publications, 2003.

[12] We needed the extra generality because our Multiyear Special Pays were more complex. We were greatly aided in this development by advice and comments from Michael Mattock and the generous provision of his code as a template.

covariates for the last two parameters to account for the effect of source of commission.

When we had the revamped program complete enough to begin estimation, we found, somewhat to our surprise, that the time required by the program to compute the fit of one parameter set was taking increasing amounts of time as the optimization continued. For example, the *optim* function required 41.4 CPU seconds per evaluation if it did only five steps in simulated annealing, but took 890 CPU seconds per evaluation for 100 steps. The problem seemed to be due to the increasing use of memory, as determined by getting memory statistics from R and by monitoring program execution with other utilities. This phenomenon obviously greatly limited both the optimization runs we could make and diagnostics on those runs. While we did get some preliminary results, our conclusion was that, in spite of its convenience, the R implementation may have reached a limit to its usefulness. We will return to this issue in the last section of this appendix.

We completed five optimization runs with our final family practice physician data set after debugging and constructing partial workarounds for the memory and runtime problems described above. All of our runs satisfied the stopping criteria of the BFGS algorithm, but the maximum over the five runs was reached when we preceded the BFGS optimization with simulated annealing, as did Mattock and Arkes. What was surprising was that the ending points of the individual runs were markedly different, indicating that the likelihood surface has a complex shape even in three dimensions, with at least several local maxima.

As we mentioned above, one advantage of the simulated annealing algorithm is that it can explore widely before settling down to a starting region for BFGS and therefore in theory avoid some multiple optima. While we found the highest maximum with this dual method, the other run beginning with simulated annealing ended up with quite different parameter estimates. Given this result and the time-consuming runs, we did not try to extend the analysis to other covariates, which would have increased the dimensionality of our search.

Table D.1 presents our estimates of the standard deviation of the shock distribution and the location and scale of the taste distribution, compared with those of Mattock and Arkes for pilots.

The three estimates produced by Mattock and Arkes derived from three separate sources for the civilian income available to pilots if they separated from the military. Figure D.1 shows the taste distribution

Table D.1
Estimated Parameters for Shock and Taste Distributions for Air Force Family Practice MDs and Pilots

	Family MD	Pilots 1	Pilots 2	Pilots 3
Shock standard deviation	$172.7K	$567K	$437K	$632K
Taste location	–$92.3K	–$144K	–$63K	-$174K
Taste scale	$16.1K	$221K	$123K	$304K

Figure D.1
Taste Distributions

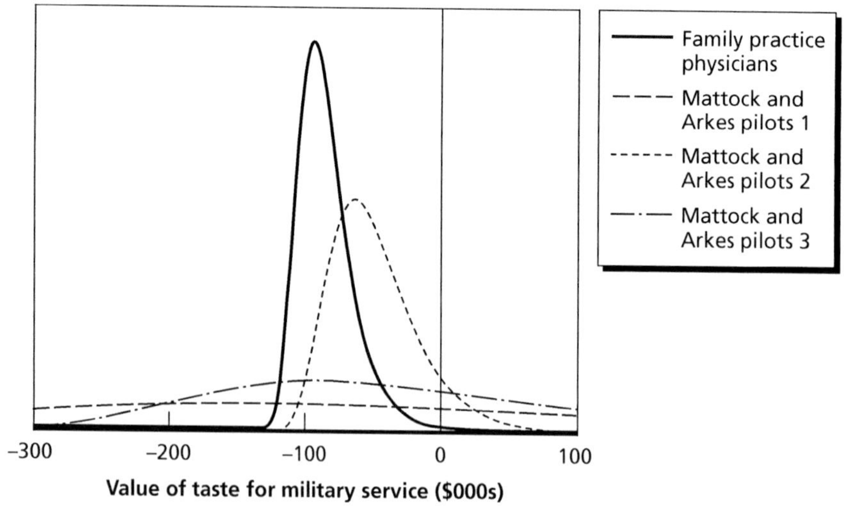

RAND *MG866-D.1*

for family practice physicians and for Mattock and Arkes' estimations of pilot taste.[13] The locations of all taste distributions are negative (i.e., military service is viewed as being less pleasant than civilian work), consistent with the previous literature. However, it is surprising that our estimate of physicians' taste distributions has a less negative location than two of the three estimated pilot taste distributions. However, the tastes for military service of the pilots are much more diffuse (have a wider range). The estimated taste of the physicians is concentrated much more closely near their center.

Figure D.2 shows the estimated distribution of shocks. The spread of the shock distributions estimated for pilots by Mattock and Arkes is substantially larger than for family practice physicians, suggesting that physicians see their career events as less variable in positive and

Figure D.2
Shock Distributions

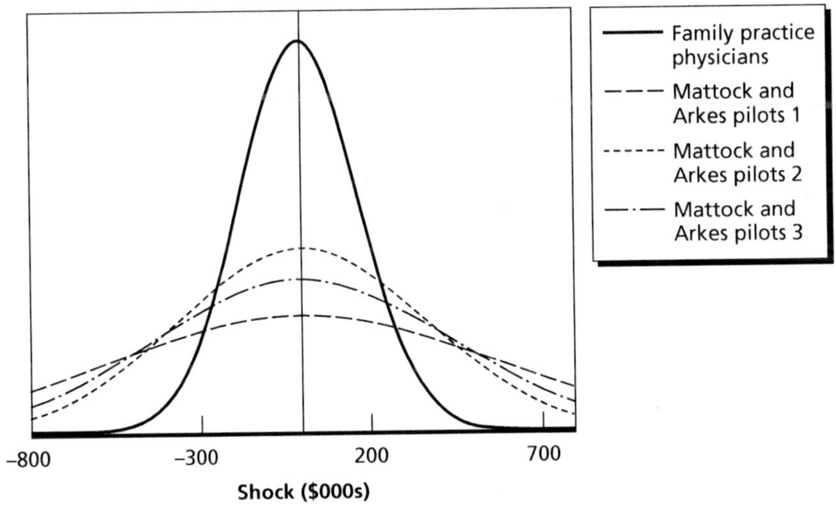

RAND *MG866-D.2*

13 The curves in Figures D.1 and D.2 are probability density curves: In Figure D.1, the area under the curve between two taste amounts is the probability that a member of that population has a taste in that range. The location of the maximum and the spread around that point are the most important characteristics, not the y-value, and so the y-axis has been omitted from these figures.

negative consequences than the aviators do. Put differently, Figure D.2 suggests family practice physicians have more predictable private-sector incomes than pilots do.

Conclusions

The theoretical basis of the DRM is still the most compelling formulation of rational decisionmaking about employment choices under uncertainty. Other, more widely used models are approximations with known and acknowledged deficiencies that have been used because of the computational demands of the DRM. The large increase in computational power has allowed us and our RAND colleagues to use an interpreted statistical language, such as R, for developing the DRM model and performing some preliminary estimations, but our experience with the physician data suggest that we may have reached the limits of R's utility for this problem. Diagnostic work on memory usage indicates that R increases its use of system resources as the optimization proceeds, eventually slowing the optimization process down to a crawl. To use the DRM further, two steps should be taken:

1. There may be some work that can be done with R's memory usage in both the DRM code itself and the *optim* function.
2. The R DRM code can be ported back to a compiled language, such as C or C++; R's structure is fairly close to that of C, which suggests that doing this would be fairly simple.

In conjunction with either of these steps, it would be helpful to explore other optimization packages and algorithms. A further useful feature would be to modify the likelihood evaluation so that the numerical integration over the taste distribution is adaptive, i.e., chooses a set of points for numerical integration that varies by integral accuracy. Currently, the integration is done over 35 points for all evaluations.

If these modifications provide better estimation performance, it would also be very useful to study how well the DRM can be estimated for various patterns of service. The pilots studied by Mattock and Arkes had a wide variety of career paths, leaving at various points in their careers. As noted in the body of this monograph, many physicians leave immediately after fulfilling their initial obligations, so we see only one decision for most physicians—at the point of leaving—which may account for some of our estimation problems. It would also be of great interest to develop estimation diagnostics for individual patterns, to try to understand if specific patterns dominate the estimation, much as is done in multivariate regression.

Other colleagues at RAND are pursuing forms of the DRM model for the military reserves. We expect that this work will provide further impetus to understanding the utility of the DRM.

References

10 U.S. Code 523, Authorized Strengths: Commissioned Officers on Active Duty in Grades of Major, Lieutenant Colonel, and Colonel and Navy Grades of Lieutenant Commander, Commander, and Captain, as amended January 3, 2007.

10 U.S. Code 2114, Students: Selection; Status; Obligation, as amended January 3, 2007.

10 U.S. Code 2123, Members of the Program: Active Duty Obligation; Failure to Complete Training; Release from Program, as amended January 3, 2007.

American Association of Medical Colleges, *AAMC Data Book: Statistical Information Related to Medical Education*, Paul Jolly and Dorothea Hudley, eds., Washington, D.C.: American Association of Medical Colleges, 1994.

American Dental Education Association, "Dental Education at a Glance," 2004. As of February 16, 2009:
http://www.adea.org/publications/adeadentaledataglance/Pages/default.aspx

Avriel, Mordecai, *Nonlinear Programming: Analysis and Methods*, Mineola, N.Y.: Dover Publications, 2003.

Brannman, Shayne, Eric W. Christensen, Ronald H. Nickel, Cori Rattelman, and Richard D. Miller, *Life-Cycle Costs of Selected Uniformed Health Professions (Phase II: The Impact of Constraints and Policies on the Optimal-Mix-of-Accession Model)*, Alexandria, Va.: Center for Naval Analyses, CRM D0007887.A2/Final, April 2003.

Brown, L. Jackson, "Dental Work Force Strategies During a Period of Change and Uncertainty," *Journal of Dental Education*, Vol. 65, No. 12, 2001.

Christakis, Nicholas A., Jerry A. Jacobs, and Carla M. Messikomer, "Changes in Self-Definition from Specialist to Generalist in a National Sample of Physicians," *Annals of Internal Medicine*, Vol. 121, No. 9, 1994.

Cohen, Daniel L., Steven J. Durning, David Cruess, and Richard MacDonald, "Longer-Term Career Outcomes of Uniformed Services University of the Health Sciences Medical School Graduates: Classes of 1980–1989," *Military Medicine*, Vol. 173, No. 5, 2008.

Daubert, Victoria L., *Retention of Volunteer Physicians in the U.S. Air Force*, Santa Monica, Calif.: RAND Corporation, R-3185-AF, February 1985. As of February 16, 2009:
http://www.rand.org/pubs/reports/R3185/

Efron, Bradley, and Tibshirani, Robert J., *An Introduction to the Bootstrap*, London: Chapman and Hall, 1993.

Gotz, Glenn A., and John J. McCall, *A Sequential Analysis of the Air Force Officer's Retirement Decision*, Santa Monica, Calif.: RAND Corporation, N-1013-1-AF, October 1979. As of February 16, 2009:
http://www.rand.org/pubs/notes/N1013-1/

Gotz, Glenn A., and John J. McCall, *A Dynamic Retention Model for Air Force Officers*, Santa Monica, Calif.: RAND Corporation, R-3028-AF, December 1984. As of February 16, 2009:
http://www.rand.org/pubs/reports/R3028/

Graubard, Barry L., and Edward L. Korn, "Predictive Margins with Survey Data," *Biometrics*, Vol. 55, June 1999, pp. 652–659.

Guay, Albert H., "Dental Practice: Prices, Production, and Profits," *Journal of the American Dental Association*, Vol. 136, No. 3, 2005.

Institute for the Measurement of Worth, Measuring Worth, Web page, 2009. As of February 16, 2009:
http://www.measuringworth.com/calculators/uscompare/

Levy, Robert A., Eric W. Christensen, and Senanu Asamoah, *Raising the Bonus and the Prospects for DOD's Attracting Fully Trained Medical Personnel*, Alexandria, Va.: Center for Naval Analyses, CRM D0013237.A2/Final, February 2006.

Mattock, Michael, and Jeremy Arkes, *The Dynamic Retention Model for Air Force Officers: New Estimates and Policy Simulations of the Aviator Continuation Pay Program*, Santa Monica, Calif.: RAND Corporation, TR-470-AF, 2007. As of February 16, 2009:
http://www.rand.org/pubs/technical_reports/TR470/

Merritt Hawkins and Associates, *2007 Review of Physician and CRNA Recruiting Incentives*, Irving, Tex.: Merritt Hawkins and Associates, 2007.

Office of the Under Secretary of Defense (Comptroller), DoD Financial Management Regulation, Volume 7A, Chapter 5, February 2002.

Office of the Under Secretary of Defense for Personnel and Readiness, "High-3 Year Average Retirement System," Web page, no date. As of February 16, 2009:
http://www.defenselink.mil/militarypay/retirement/ad/03_highthree.html

Philpott, Tom, "Surgeon General: Looming Doctor Shortage," *Stars and Stripes*, July 13, 2006. As of February 16, 2009:
http://www.military.com/features/0,15240,105400,00.html

R Development Core Team, The R Project for Statistical Computing, Web site, no date. As of February 16, 2009:
http://www.r-project.org/

Rostker, Bernard, *I Want You! The Evolution of the All-Volunteer Force*, Santa Monica, Calif.: RAND Corporation, MG-265-RC, 2006. As of February 16, 2009:
http://www.rand.org/pubs/monographs/MG265/

Starr, Paul, *The Social Transformation of American Medicine*, New York: Basic Books, 1982.

Uniformed Services Almanac, Falls Church, Va.: Uniformed Services Almanac, Inc., 2008 and earlier years.

U.S. Air Force Personnel Center, Air Force Personnel Statistics, Web page, 2009. As of February 16, 2009:
http://wwa.afpc.randolph.af.mil/demographics/reportsearch.asp

U.S. Department of the Air Force, *Active Duty Service Commitments*, Air Force Instruction 36-2107, April 22, 2005. As of February 16, 2009:
http://www.e-publishing.af.mil/shared/media/epubs/AFI36-2107.pdf

U.S. Department of Commerce, Bureau of Economic Analysis, National Economic Accounts, May 16, 2008. As of February 24, 2009:
http://www.bea.gov/national/nipaweb/SelectTable.asp?Selected=N

U.S. Department of Defense, *Financial Management Regulation, Volume 7A*, Chapter 5, November 2008. As of February 16, 2009:
http://www.defenselink.mil/comptroller/fmr/07a/07a_05.pdf

U.S. Department of Health and Human Services, *Personnel Manual*, Chapter CC22: Pay and Allowance Administration, Subchapter CC22.2: Special Pays, PHS-CC 637, November 10, 1998. As of February 16, 2009:
http://dcp.psc.gov/eccis/documents/CCPM22_2_10.pdf

———, Health Resources and Services Administration, National Center for Health Workforce Analysis, U.S. Health Workforce Personnel Factbook, Web page, no date. As of February 16, 2009:
http://bhpr.hrsa.gov/healthworkforce/reports/factbook.htm

U.S. Department of Labor, Bureau of Labor Statistics, Occupational Employment Statistics, "Occupational Employment and Wages, May 2007," Web page, April 2008. As of February 16, 2009:
http://www.bls.gov/OES/current/oes291024.htm

U.S. General Accounting Office, *Military Physicians: DOD's Medical School and Scholarship Program*, GAO/HEHS-95-244, September 1995. As of February 16, 2009:
http://www.gao.gov/cgi-bin/getrpt?GAO/HEHS-95-244

Warner, John T., *Military Compensation and Retention: An Analysis of Alternative Models and a Simulation of a New Retention Model*, Washington, D.C.: The Center for Naval Analyses, 1981.

Weeks, William B., and Amy E. Wallace, "Long-Term Financial Implications of Specialty Training for Physicians," *American Journal of Medicine*, Vol. 113, No. 5, 2002.

Weeks, William B., and Amy E. Wallace, "Time and Money: A Retrospective Evaluation of the Inputs, Outputs, and Incomes of Physicians," *Archives of Internal Medicine*, Vol. 163, No. 8, 2003.